THE ASSASSINATION OF TROTSKY

NICHOLAS MOSLEY

Nicholas Mosley is the author of several highly praised novels including ACCIDENT, IMPOSSIBLE OBJECT and NATALIE NATALIA. He has also written for the cinema and was commissioned to write the screenplay for Joseph Losey's film of THE ASSASSINATION OF TROTSKY.

NICHOLAS MOSLEY

THE ASSASSINATION
OF TROTSKY

published by Sphere Books Ltd
30/32, Gray's Inn Road, London, WC1X 8JL

First published in Great Britain in 1972
by Michael Joseph Ltd.
Copyright © 1972 by Josef Shaftel Productions
First Abacus edition: 1972

Printed in Great Britain by Hazell Watson & Viney Ltd
Aylesbury, Bucks

EVENTS

1879 Trotsky born on 26th October in the southern Ukraine, the son of a prosperous Jewish farmer called Bronstein.

1888–98 At schools in Odessa and Nikolayev. Becomes involved in revolutionary student politics.

1898 Arrested and sent to Siberia. Marries Alexandra Sokolovskaya. Two daughters born in Siberia.

1902 Escapes and makes his way to London. Joins Lenin and other revolutionary *émigrés*. Meets Natalya Sedova.

1903 Communist Party Congress in Brussels. Split between Bolsheviks (Lenin) and Mensheviks (Trotsky).

1905 Abortive revolution in Russia. Trotsky in St Petersburg. Becomes chairman of the St Petersburg Soviet.

1905–7 Second imprisonment and exile to Siberia. Trotsky's and Natalya's son Lyova born.

1907 Second escape. Trotsky rejoins Natalya in St Petersburg.

1907–17 Trotsky and Natalya and two sons (Sergei born in 1908) move between London, Vienna, Berlin, Paris, Zurich and New York.

1914 First World War begins.
    Ramon Mercader born in Barcelona.

1917 February. Successful revolution against the Tsar in Russia. Government of liberals and moderate socialists.
    May. Trotsky arrives in Petrograd.
    October. Bolshevik revolution. Lenin and Trotsky take over power.

1918 Trotsky as Foreign Minister. Peace talks with the Germans at Brest Litovsk.

1918–20	Civil War in Russia. Trotsky as organiser and Commander-in-Chief of the victorious Red Army.
1924	Death of Lenin.
1924–6	Struggle for power between Lenin's successors. Stalin, Zinoviev and Kamenev form a bloc to keep out Trotsky.
1926–8	Stalin takes over supreme control in Russia. Trotsky is active in opposition.
1928	Stalin exiles Trotsky to Alma Ata.
1929	Trotsky exiled from Russian territory. He moves to the island of Prinkipo, near Constantinople.
1930–3	Trotsky writes his *Autobiography* and his *History of the Russian Revolution*. Stalin forces industrialisation and collectivisation on Russia. Trotsky's daughter Zina commits suicide.
1933	Hitler in power in Germany.
1933–5	Trotsky in France. Ill-health.
1935	Trotsky in Norway. He writes *The Revolution Betrayed* – an indictment of Stalin's bureaucracy. Stalin begins his purges in Russia. First of the Moscow show-trials in which leading Bolsheviks confess to having betrayed and sabotaged Communism under orders from Trotsky. Trotsky and his son Lyova deny charges.
1936	Start of Spanish Civil War. Ramon Mercader joins the Republican Army. He is sent to a school for terrorists.
1937	Trotsky sails for Mexico, having been granted asylum by President Cardenas. He lives in the house of Diego Rivera, the painter. Trotsky's second son, Sergei, disappears in the Russian purges.
1937–8	Further show-trials in Moscow. Leaders of the Bolshevik Party, the Red Army and the Civil Service are shot. Mass purges.

1937–8	Trotsky is cleared of all charges made against him at the trials by an investigating committee under the chairmanship of John Dewey, the American philosopher.
1938	The Founding Conference in Paris of Trotsky's Fourth International – an organisation of workers to stand for socialist principles in opposition to Stalin's Comintern. Ramon Mercader, alias Jacques Mornard, comes to Paris where he is introduced to Sylvia Agelof. Sylvia is working as an interpreter for the Fourth International.
	Death in Paris of Lyova, Trotsky's eldest son.
	Murder of Rudolf Klement, secretary to the Fourth International.
1939	Trotsky moves to the house in the Avenue Viena in Coyoacan on the outskirts of Mexico City. He fortifies the house against threats of assassination. He is protected by five or six secretaries or guards.
	His grandson Seva, son of his daughter Zina, comes to join Trotsky and Natalya at Coyoacan.
	August. The Stalin-Hitler pact.
	September. Outbreak of Second World War.
	Ramon Mercader, alias Jacques Mornard, alias Frank Jacson, arrives in Mexico City.
1940	Sylvia Agelof arrives in Mexico. She joins Jacques Mornard. She visits the house at Coyoacan, where she is welcomed as a loyal Trotskyite.
	May 24th. First assassination attempt against Trotsky: David Alfaro Siqueiros, the painter, leads a gang of fellow-artists, Mexican Stalinists and ex-Spanish Civil War veterans; they break into Trotsky's house at night; they fire several hundred rounds from machine-guns into his bedroom; Trotsky emerges unscathed.
	May-August. Claims by the Mexican Communist Party that the raid was a put-up job organised by Trotsky. Trotsky's denials.

1940   Sylvia Agelof and Jacques Mornard are together in Mexico City. Jacques Mornard has become friendly with Trotsky's guards. He is invited into the house at Coyoacan, as Sylvia's friend.

August 17th. Jacques Mornard, alias Ramon Mercader, is alone with Trotsky in his study. He appears to be ill, and leaves.

August 20th. Ramon Mercader is again alone with Trotsky. He takes an ice-pick from beneath his raincoat and drives it into Trotsky's skull.

August 21st. Trotsky dies.

"Trotskyists learned the rhythm of history . . . to subordinate their individual tastes to the laws of history."

"I can say that I live on this earth not in accordance with the rule, but as an exception to the rule."

"There is an irony deep laid in the very relations of life. It is the duty of the historian as of the artist to bring it to the surface."

"It is certainly victims that move humanity forward."

TROTSKY

Chapter 1

In May 1940 the Germans were overrunning Europe: they were spreading one form of National Socialism or Nazism; their allies, the Russians, had annexed parts of Poland and Finland and were spreading their own brand of socialism or Communism; these two ideologies which their protagonists insisted correctly were so different but which to cynics in the third and so-called democratic camp appeared in their ruthlessness so similar had come together, in the Russian-German pact of 1939, as if in mockery of themselves and to prove the cynics right. The old order in Europe was going down before an onslaught of which the common characteristic seemed to be just cynicism. With the destruction of old traditions and beliefs, the manipulation of power seemed the only reality.

In May 1940 Trotsky was living in a fortified house in Coyoacan, a suburb of Mexico City. In 1917 he had been a leader of the Russian Revolution; then for six years he had been second in power in Russia only to Lenin; when Lenin had died he had had a chance to take over power but had let the opportunity slip and the leadership had passed to Stalin. Stalin was an arch manipulator of power: Trotsky, for all his ruthlessness, was never cynical. From 1926 on Stalin had edged Trotsky further and further out of power until, in 1929, he had exiled him to Turkey. For a while Trotsky flourished there with his writing and polemics; then under pressure from Stalin again he was hounded through Europe while his followers in Russia and indeed almost everyone who could have rivalled Stalin anywhere were killed. In 1937 Trotsky landed in Mexico and built fortifications round his house. He was the last survivor of Stalin's terror. Mexico was a socialist state but with a lively tradition of anarchy, and it was the only country in the world to offer him asylum.

Trotsky's view of the war in 1940 was that in principle it did not matter to whom Russia was allied, this was wholly a matter of expediency. Both the Nazis and the Western Powers fought for the interests only of their own ruling class: the war was "a struggle between imperialist slave-holders of different camps for a new division of the world". In politics, Trotsky said, there were no "eternal morals": means were subordinated to an end and the end, for a Marxist, was the establishment of the true workers' state. This was a matter, Marxists believed, of history. The triumph of the proletariat was the way not in which history ought to be going but in which it was going, and to fit in with this was the best anyone could do – this was "scientific"; in some sense even "moral".

Trotsky, exiled in Mexico, had kept his Marxist faith in the way history was going but he had also – and seemed to have had from the beginning – an ironic view of events that in fact occurred apart from those that were supposed to occur. In 1940 the dictatorship of Stalin was in alliance with the dictatorship of Hitler; there was no sign of the triumph of the true workers' state either here or in the camp of the dictators' opponents, the Western democracies. Trotsky saw this; railed against it. Some of his followers in America argued that they should wash their hands of the war – all manipulators of power were logically as bad as the Nazis, they said, so there was no side on which to fight. But there was a part of Trotsky that worked not by logic but by instinct: when asked by a follower in 1940 what a Trotskyite in America should do if he were drafted into the army, he replied "Let him be drafted; I don't think he should try to avoid the draft – he must go with his generation and participate in its life." He had a feeling for life beyond a respect for logic.

In 1932, writing about the way in which the Communist

Revolution had not in fact followed the course predicted by Marx, he had said "But history is full of such paradoxes. Pedants think that the dialectic is an idle play of the mind. In reality it only reproduces the process of evolution, which lives and moves by way of contradictions."

Trotsky is one of the few Marxist writers who seem to have a feel of the meaning of dialectics. Marx called his theory "dialectical materialism" and the "materialism" is not hard to understand but "dialectical" seems often to be used in a sense little different from "able to be investigated by reasonable argument". Trotsky sometimes used the word in this sense – though when he was in his pedantic vein he usually used the word 'scientific' – but he also used dialectical in its profound sense of referring to the processes of change and of growth in life; of things being seen in their context not absolutely but relatively; of the play of opposites and contradictions of which an understanding is necessary for any true insight into nature. To understand this there is no place for cynicism; but perhaps for irony. A person has to be able to stand back from himself to perceive paradoxes; it is by doing this that he can best describe the processes of growth. This was not an attribute of Stalinism, which depended on the simplicity of violence.

In the summer of 1940 there were two attempts to assassinate Trotsky – the first, in May, by a gang of ex-Spanish Civil War veterans who broke into Trotsky's house at night and fired hundreds of rounds from machine-guns into his bedroom. This failed. The second was in August, and was made by an individual who was almost certainly a Stalinist agent and who was invited by Trotsky himself into his study. This attempt succeeded. On each occasion there were mysteries – in the first, the questions of how the raiders got in, why no opposition was put up, how Trotsky had escaped so miraculously from such a barrage. In the second there were again the questions of why the assassin had been let in; also this time the riddle of his identity. The assassin today (1972) is said to be alive and well in Prague or Moscow;

but although he was in prison for twenty years no one knows who he really is, and he does not admit his own identity.

Trotsky is one of the most identifiable characters in history – a man of action, a soldier, a political and military leader at a place and time – Petrograd 1917 – where the fate of the world hung in the balance: also a thinker, a writer, who carried on a commentary brilliantly throughout his life on his own actions and the drama of the huge events around him. He not only led a revolution, created an army, won a war; he evolved theories to describe social processes and had a literary output that would fill thirty volumes. And yet – or because of this – it is impossible to pin him down: with a personality so big and a life so full Trotsky cannot be tabulated; the processes of such energy can only be described in 'dialectics'. Some of Trotsky's enormous literary output is written in a style of pedantic Marxist jargon: much of it is written with passionate wit and irony. But whatever his style it is never – in his words – "that purely individual irony that spreads itself out like a smoke of indifference over the whole effort and intention of mankind": it is always, rather, the "irony deep-laid in the very relations of life". Whatever contradictions Trotsky contained, he was never indifferent. He cared, and cared violently, for "the whole effort and intention of mankind" – even when his writing had the rhetoric of a schoolboy slanging-match. He cared for mankind, ultimately, more than for dogmatic Marxism: it was this care that he gave his life to, gave up power for, and which in the end probably killed him. He was never less than a passionate Marxist; only greater.

The story of this book takes place between the first assassination attempt in May 1940 and the second in August – by which time the Europe that Trotsky had cared about so much seemed to be in danger also of dying. But Trotsky always thought his ideas would in some sense be victorious. Interspersed in this book there are chapters which try to say who Trotsky was and what he had done and what he believed in, without which his personal drama has no meaning. The book is not a biography – this has been done at length and brilliantly by Isaac Deutscher. This book is more an effort at interpretation.

In 1940 Trotsky was an old man living under protection in Mexico City. He was guarded by American college boys: his words, which he still poured out, reached fewer and fewer people; they were listened to by less. Around him was the war which was to involve the whole world and make a nonsense of many of his predictions. Yet Stalin, in supreme power in Russia, went to enormous trouble to kill him. If Trotsky possessed no power he was still powerful as a symbol – and as such he was a profound enemy of Stalin's. And today, too, he has this authority. What exactly this is, as is proper with symbols, is what is hard to pin down: his authority is both to do with his actions and theories and yet it goes deeper – it is as if his effects continued in a different area from many of his intentions. He was a politician: he did not want to be a prophet. But he himself glimpsed something profound in the ironies of history when towards the end of his life he wrote that it might soon have to be recognised that "the socialist programme based on the internal contradictions of a capitalist society, had petered out as a Utopia": however in this event a "minimum programme would still be required – to defend the interests of the slaves of the totalitarian bureaucratic system". It is in some such protestation as this that Trotsky's importance still lies, as perhaps it did at the end of his life. He was a passionate fighter for a true workers' state – which struggle, though Utopian, is nevertheless a necessity for mankind: he was a passionate fighter for the poor and underprivileged – which effort, though paradoxical (there always seems to be someone underprivileged as the cost of another's achievement) is also a vital and often effective necessity for mankind: but above all he could view the whole difficult business not only with austere seriousness but also with good-humour and detachment – and this is perhaps a greater, and rarer, necessity for mankind – because as Trotsky so often said it is to do with the processes of life and growth and change. And by being able to do this he created a liveliness not only in his work but in his personality and story. This will last. He is a prototype, that is, for all passionate fighters who fight and know socially the odds against them but who still show their faith in the world by just protesting this faith. This was why Stalin had to have Trotsky killed; because the power at the hands of the manipulator is ultimately just death, and the style of the dialectician is life and thus the enemy. And perhaps this was why Trotsky even while going down beneath the blow of the assassin was heard to claim that he had prevented him.

Chapter 2

Trotsky was born on 26th October, 1879, at Yanovka near Brobinetz in the southern Ukraine. He was the son of a prospering Jewish farmer called Bronstein. He was named Leon Davidovitch. Jews in Russia did not often escape from cramped town life, but they had been offered land on the uninhabited steppe earlier in the century by the Tsar and Trotsky's father had taken on six hundred and fifty acres. Trotsky's childhood was hard-working and austere, but not grim. He remembered it as "the greyish childhood of a lower-middle-class family, spent in a village in an obscure corner where nature is wide and manners, views and interests are narrow". But he had idyllic memories of the harvesting, threshing, birds-nesting, and hunting marmots; the long winter evenings with the family round the fire reading aloud or playing Old Maid. His impressions of his childhood in his Autobiography are an odd mixture of appreciation and faint reproach.

Some of his earliest memories were of the predicament of the farm labourers who lived on a diet of soup and porridge. One day they demonstrated in Trotsky's father's yard to ask for more food. They lay silently face down on the ground and raised their cracked feet in the air.

Another of Trotsky's memories was of the same labourers giving a performance of a mime-show called "Czar Maximilian". He wrote – "For the first time a fantastic world was revealed to me, a world transformed into a theatrical reality".

Trotsky went to school in Odessa, where he lodged with his mother's cousin. He studied science, mathematics, German and French. Odessa was a cosmopolitan seaside port and Trotsky learned more than just a schoolboy's curriculum: he was introduced to Russian and European literature; he began to compose his own verses and was persuaded by the grown-ups to read them aloud. Embarrassed, yet receiving admiration, he felt he had "tasted of the tree of knowledge". His cousin was a translator and a writer of children's stories: the school had been founded by Lutherans originally for middle-class German residents. The first day Trotsky went there, dressed in his school uniform, he was spat at by the odd-job boy in the hall. Trotsky raged; but recognised the boy was "venting his sense of social protest". He worked hard and did well: the discipline in his cousin's home and in the school was strict. Also Odessa was "perhaps the most police-ridden city in police-ridden Russia". Trotsky liked getting back to the country where he rode, played games, flirted. In the town he loved the theatre and the opera: he plunged into the world of books. He wrote – "The awakened hunger to see, to know, to absorb, found relief in this insatiable swallowing of printed matter".

When he was sixteen he graduated to the provincial college at Nikolayev. There he came into contact with revolutionary students. He brought with him a sense of protest – a "sympathy for the downtrodden and indignation over injustice" – but he had no regard yet for "socialist Utopias". What haunted him was the complexity of his emotions about life in country and town – the ways in which on the farm his father had close physical contact with his labourers and yet there was no proper feeling between them; how in the town in spite of sophistication there was scarcely any contact between different groups at all – everyone stayed within the confines of their business. Trotsky admired his father, yet was opposed to his acceptance of things as they were. He wanted change – and a theory to explain change. He wrote – "The dull empiricism, the unashamed, cringing worship of the fact which is so often only imaginary, and falsely interpreted at that, became odious to me. Beyond the facts, I looked for laws. I felt that I could move and act only when I held in my hand the thread of the general".

In Nikolayev the revolutionary students were divided between Marxists and Narodniks – the former advocating revolution through the organisation of industrial workers, and the latter advocating alternately peaceful change through education and, when this failed, terrorism and violence. Trotsky still had hardly heard of Marx: by temperament he became a Narodnik. He and the other students met in the garden of a fruitgrower called Shvigovsky: there, beneath apple-trees, they argued into the night. Trotsky left the lodgings recommended by his father and moved in with Shvigovsky and five other students: they led a communal life, all wearing "blue smocks and round straw hats" and carrying "black canes". Their first object for enlightenment was a labourer who worked in Shvigovsky's orchard. He, as so often happened in Trotsky's life, turned out be an agent of the police.

In 1896 there were strikes in many towns in Russia; in St Petersburg a woman student called Vetrova burned herself to death. Trotsky recalled – "I started my revolutionary work to the accompaniment of the Vetrova demonstration". The up-heavals were against the whole dead weight of established society; revolution was in the air. There were one or two factories around Nikolayev: Trotsky and his friends wrote articles encouraging the workers to strike, sat up at night writing pamphlets in longhand and printing them on primitive machinery. They distributed the pamphlets to the workers who "turned towards us as if they had been waiting for this". Trotsky felt his power with words over readers who "pictured the author as a strange and mighty person". The students worked hectically, and the workers listened.

One day Trotsky was handing on a bundle of pamphlets to a colleague whom he had met behind a cemetery: the colleague, as usual, turned out to be an agent of the police: and Trotsky and hundreds of his co-workers were arrested.

21

Trotsky spent a large part of his early manhood in prison; this did not seem to worry him much; during his second spell in jail in 1906 he even said that he left solitary confinement in St Petersburg "with a tinge of regret; it was so quiet there, so eventless, so perfect for intellectual work". During his first imprisonment conditions were not so ideal. For three weeks he was in a cell where he and the one other inmate had to keep pressed together to stay warm: then he was in solitary confinement for three months in a cell crawling with vermin and with no ventilation: only after this was he moved to another prison where, with the use of the prison library, he spent a year reading the Gospels in four languages and wrote a thousand-page treatise on Freemasonry. He also evolved a system whereby he could share his intellectual activities with other prisoners by tapping messages in code through the walls, and by tying up bundles of manuscript and swinging them from cell-window to cell-window by means of broom-handles and bits of string.

One of the students arrested with him was Alexandria Soko-lovskaya, a girl six years older than himself and a Marxist who had been his leading opponent in the arguments beneath the apple-trees. Trotsky, still a Narodnik believing in reform by education or violence, had argued with her passionately: he had once shouted "a curse upon all Marxists and upon those who want to bring dryness and hardness into all relations of life!" Sokolovskaya had left the meeting in a rage. Later, she and Trotsky married. His own description of Alexandria Soko-lovskaya and of his marriage reads: "Her utter loyalty to socialism and her complete lack of any personal ambition gave her unquestioned moral authority. The work that we were doing bound us closely together, and so, to avoid being separated, we were married in the transfer prison in Moscow."

He and his wife were sent to Siberia where they lived in a small village on the river Lena where the temperature in winter was 35 degrees below zero and where in the summer the midges were so bad that they could bite cows to death. Here Trotsky studied

22

Marx, reading by candlelight and brushing cockroaches off the pages. The only way to get rid of the cockroaches finally was to move out of the hut for a day or two and leave the door open in the temperature of 35 below zero.

The exiles carried on their revolutionary schooling in Siberia; they exchanged pamphlets, books and letters by hand and by post; there was still a feeling of intense activity. One of the peculiarities of the Tsarist penal system was the way in which the authorities sent revolutionaries to be together in Siberia almost as if to universities. Trotsky began writing for a Narodnik newspaper under the pen name of "Antid Oto" – a play on the word "antidote". A peculiarity of revolutionary activity was the way in which people got in the habit of using names other than their own. In his early years Leon Davidovitch Bronstein was known by many names – Antid Oto, Pero, Petr Petrovitch – and finally Trotsky.

In the summer of 1902 he received by the underground post a Marxist newspaper, *Iskra*, which was being printed in London; also a book by Lenin who was in London called *What is to be done?* This excited Trotsky so much that he determined to escape: he said goodbye to Alexandria Sokolovskaya and the two small daughters which had been born to them; he left a dummy in his bed and hid under the hay of a friendly peasant's cart who drove him back towards civilisation. He passed the time under the hay reading the *Iliad*. He had acquired a false passport on which he had written, on the spur of the moment, the name of one of his guards – Trotsky.

After a journey on false papers and being smuggled through Samara, Karkov, Vienna, Zurich and Paris, he reached London. Early one October morning he took a cab to the house in Bloomsbury where Lenin lived. Lenin was still in bed. Trotsky remembered – "The kindly expression on his face was tinged with justifiable amazement." Lenin welcomed Trotsky, took him around London, introduced him to other revolutionaries. Trotsky remembered the way in which Lenin pointed out to him London landmarks – "That is *their* Westminster Abbey"; "That is where *they* do such and such". "They" were not the English but the ruling class – the enemy. On his own, Trotsky had difficulty in finding his way round London: he remarked – "With my usual penchant for systematic thinking, I called this defect 'topographical cretinism'."

In London there were a small group of revolutionaries round Lenin – his wife Krupskaya, Martov, Plekhanov, Vera Zasulitch. They wrote pamphlets and articles for *Iskra*; Krupskaya decoded messages in invisible ink over the gas fire. Lenin spent much of his time in the library of the British Museum; he was studying economics and history. There was an extraordinary air of confidence about this small group at this time; they believed like religious fanatics that they were instruments of destiny. Also like fanatics, they quarrelled. The dispute at the time was superficially about who was to have practical control of *Iskra*; more deeply it was about the whole theory of socialist organisation – whether control should be vested in a tight-knit group or even in an individual where it might be effective, or whether it should be diffused in the form of a committee of party-members chosen by seniority. Beneath this argument about principle were personal animosities; the older generation of revolutionaries did not approve of the younger; Plekhanov disliked Trotsky; Trotsky for a time was hostile to Lenin. In these quarrels the personal animosities were for the most part cloaked by grandiose political jargon. Trotsky used homely language. He referred to Lenin as "a slovenly attorney", a "vulgar farce", and "morally repulsive". Lenin, always more cautious, replied that Trotsky was a "hollow bell".

The quarrel came to a head at the Communist Party Congress in Brussels in 1903. Here the disputants – meeting in a flea-ridden store-room of a friendly co-operative society – all became infected with irritation. They split into two camps – the Bolsheviks ("men of the majority") and Mensheviks ("men of the minority"). The Bolsheviks were the advocates of tight-knit control and the

Mensheviks were the advocates of broad committees. The names with which they were labelled thus had nothing to do with their convictions, however bitter the quarrels, but simply with the fact that, when it came to a vote, the Bolsheviks had won and the Mensheviks had lost. This, above everything, was what mattered in party politics.

Trotsky was a leader of the Mensheviks – he believed in the power of argument in large committees. Lenin, who hoped that power might be effective, was leader of the Bolsheviks. The debates were carried on with a mixture of theoretical argument and savage insult. Even Lenin wrote afterwards "I am aware that often I acted and behaved with terrible irritation"; also "I am willing to admit my guilt to anyone". This, perhaps, was one of the sources of his strength: he also convinced by being inscrutable and biding his time. Trotsky became carried away by his skill and style with words: he thought that a job was over when an argument had been won.

Trotsky left Brussels in some disillusionment: he thought "everybody was merely groping about and working with impalpable things". Lenin himself after the Congress was ill for weeks. Trotsky thought that Lenin's behaviour in trying to get rid of older party members was "horrible and outrageous": yet at the same time "politically it was right and necessary". Trotsky, as a portent of his future dramatic behaviour, could see no way through this dilemma except first by withdrawal and then by a plunge into extrovert action. For a while he dissociated himself from both sides of the party; then he was the first of the *émigré* revolutionaries to arrive in St Petersburg for the abortive revolution of 1905.

This had begun when Father Gapon, a priest, had led a peaceful demonstration to the seat of government at the Winter Palace and the police had fired into the crowd. The crowd had fought back. The revolution had settled down by the time Trotsky arrived into a stalemate in which the St Petersburg Soviet, or committee of workers, had control of much of the town but the

Tsarist forces, the police and the army, were waiting on the outskirts trusting to the apathy of the Russian masses and their ultimate tradition of obedience. Trotsky became chairman of the St Petersburg Soviet; he made fiery speeches, poured out pamphlets, demonstrated in dress-rehearsal the practice of revolutionary control. The other Communist leaders including Lenin arrived in St Petersburg only just before the end of the revolution; they looked on Trotsky with a mixture of genuine admiration and yet perhaps the feeling that they could let him be a scapegoat. At the end of the year the soldiers and police moved in on the Soviet; Trotsky, in the chair at the meeting, wittily insisted that the officer should wait for permission before he took the floor: the officer obeyed for a while, then led Trotsky off to jail.

His second period in prison, Trotsky said, was much easier to bear than his first: he had gained confidence as a revolutionary, he had become a leader, and he wanted to do a lot of reading. He found his compulsory walks in the prison yard annoying because they interfered with his writing of a pamphlet which attacked liberalism. A fellow-prisoner remembered – "Trotsky's prison cell soon became transformed into a sort of library. He was supplied with all the new books that deserved attention; he read them all, the entire day, from morning till late at night. 'I feel splendid,' he would say: 'I sit and work and feel perfectly sure that I can't be arrested. You will agree that in Tsarist Russia this is rather an unusual sensation'."

He was again sentenced to exile in Siberia. In January 1907 he started the journey. Fifty-two soldiers guarded fourteen prisoners. The journey to a base-camp took thirty-three days by train and sleigh and on foot. Then at the base-camp Trotsky was taught by a revolutionary doctor how to simulate sciatica. He was left behind at the base hospital to wait for the next party. He bribed a drunken sleigh driver to take him to another settlement hundreds of miles to the west where there was a railway line. He kept the driver awake by pulling

26

his cap off in the icy cold. He was back in St Petersburg in eleven days.

The period between the abortive revolution of 1905 and the revolution in 1917 was comparatively uneventful in Trotsky's life. He moved between London, Vienna, Berlin, Paris, Zurich and New York. He edited a newspaper in Vienna and became a war correspondent in the Balkans. He wrote tracts and articles analysing the untimeliness of the 1905 revolution and preparing for the next. He had no doubt that it would come.

The confidence of the tiny bands of revolutionaries at this time seemed to have impressed even the ranks of their opponents: in spite of the massive power of the army and police and the continuing apathy of the masses the sense of revolution in the air was inescapable; this was noticeable in the extraordinary way in which the revolutionaries appeared to be allowed to move in and out of Russia; were almost allowed to escape, it seemed, if they had the energy and will to do so. Trotsky wrote – "Officials treated us with the utmost consideration: revolution and counter-revolution were still in the balance and no one knew which side would win." In spite of all the violence and repression there did seem to be some acceptance of coming defeat amongst the authorities – they had lost confidence – this was to be demonstrated, cataclysmically, in the war of 1914. This was a time when the upper and middle classes of Europe had reached a condition of unparalleled prosperity; they had created a golden world on an exhausted bed of exploitation; and a lot of young men wanted to rush out and die. At first the young men from the golden world even thought life happy in the trenches. There was some sense in the revolutionaries' confidence that they only had to wait, and history would fall into their lap like a rotten apple.

Thirty-five years later, when the second world war had begun and Trotsky was living in Mexico, there was no rush to the colours; no more belief in the glories of war; not much illusion, even, that the true workers' state might just be round the corner.

27

But there was still, with Trotsky at least, the old almost crazy-seeming confidence. This was no longer a short-term political confidence: it was a long-term insistence about the nature of man: but it had something of the same courage in the face of the venomous and often ludicrous circumstances of the outside world. Stalin was out to kill him. Trotsky knew this. Stalin had been saying that Trotsky was in league with Hitler: recently he, Stalin, had made a pact with Hitler, so now he had now to say that Trotsky was in league with the United States. None of it made sense: but this senselessness was part of what Trotsky spoke out against, so Stalin had to kill him. Trotsky lived in his fortified house in Coyoacan and looked back on a life in which there had been many incidents both brutal and ludicrous; but nevertheless he had to keep going. He had with him his second wife Natalya Sedova whom he had married (or rather had simply called her his wife) in 1903. He had met her in Paris where she, a student of art, had taken him round the Louvre. Then he had not appreciated art; Rubens for instance had seemed to him "too well-fed and satisfied". Now Natalya had been with him for thirty-seven years: in his last will and testament he had said how he loved not only Natalya, but everything in life that was beautiful.

Chapter 3

In May 1940 Trotsky was sixty years old. He suffered from occasional bouts of illness. Natalya wrote – "Sometimes I heard Lev Davidovitch, when alone, say from his innermost depths 'I am tired . . . tired'." But for the most part he radiated vitality and energy.

He was above medium height, with a broad chest and thin legs. He had an immensely high forehead with thick grey hair and deep blue eyes. When he tried to travel incognito he would sometimes shave off his goatee beard and part his hair in the middle; but crowds would recognise him and call out "Trotsky! Trotsky!"

He was accustomed to working at least twelve hours a day, writing and dictating to his secretaries. When he went on outings to the mountains round Mexico City he would walk at such a pace that he left his young bodyguard behind; then he would reappear carrying enormous cacti to add to the collection in his garden.

The house at Coyoacan was in an ordinary Mexican suburb at the corner of Viena Avenue and Morelos Street set in its own garden with a wall round it heightened to keep out intruders. There was one watchtower and, before the events of May, just a primitive system of trip-wires and alarm bells. One side of the garden shared a wall with the adjoining property; beyond another was a high bank almost overlooking it beyond which again there was a canal. The other two walls separated the property from streets which were stony and dusty in the dry season and which in the rainy season turned to mud. Coyoacan had been where Cortes had set up his headquarters in the sixteenth century when attacking Montezuma in Mexico City; the city at that time was built on islands in the middle of a lake crossed only by causeways; Coyoacan was on high ground at the edge. In 1940 it was a quiet and slightly derelict area, not yet incorporated into the later more prosperous suburbs.

Trotsky lived a life of rigorous routine. He got up at seven-fifteen and worked in the garden tending his rabbits and chickens for an hour till breakfast. The feed of the rabbits and chickens was prepared, his secretary said, "according to the most scientific formula he could obtain". After breakfast he wrote and dictated until lunch. He spent as little time as possible at meals during the day: his secretary remembered – "I could not say that I ever noticed on his face any mark of enjoyment for what he ate and drank." He himself referred to – "Eating, dressing, all these miserable little things that have to be repeated every day." He was such a martinet about the correct scientific methods of washing-up that people had to ask him not to do it. After lunch he rested for an hour; then was ready to receive visitors. But he "hated pointless conversations and unannounced visits" and "any unmotivated disturbance irritated him extremely". He would later have another look at his garden and rabbits and chickens, and work again till supper. This was the one meal at which he did relax: it would be a family occasion with the guards and secretaries round the table: Trotsky would tell anecdotes or lead discussions – nearly always about politics. Then he would work again until it was time for bed.

Living in the house with him at this time were Natalya; his grandson Estaban or Seva – the son of Trotsky's daughter Zina and her husband Platon Volkov – and six guards, or secretaries, who took turns in manning the watchtower and in typing from Trotsky's dictation. These secretaries and guards were mostly Americans; there was one German, Otto Schuessler. Trotsky had a considerable following in America in 1940 mainly concentrated amongst New York intelligentsia and certain mid-west Unions. Also in the house at the time were three Mexican servants – a cook, a parlourmaid and a gardener – and two old friends and colleagues of Trotsky's from Paris, Alfred and Marguerite Rosmer.

When Trotsky had first come to Mexico in January 1937 he had been a guest in the house of Diego Rivera, the painter. Rivera had been a founder member of the Mexican Communist Party: during the thirties he had fallen out with the Stalinists and had backed Trotsky; he had been instrumental in encouraging President Cardenas to grant Trotsky asylum in Mexico. Trotsky and Natalya had lived in proximity with Rivera and his wife Frida Kahlo for two years; then they had fallen out, and saw no more of each other. The quarrel had been partly political – Rivera had broken with the Communist Party and was backing a rival right-wing candidate for the Mexican presidency against Cardenas – but also personal; Trotsky was said to have flirted with Rivera's wife.

The house in Viena Avenue was the first freehold Trotsky ever owned; also the last. He had begun by renting the house, but there had been rumours that Stalinist Communists were trying to buy it to turn Trotsky out, so it was bought for him by money raised amongst his followers in America.

Stalin's pursuit and persecution of Trotsky in Mexico makes little sense in terms of a practical power-struggle: Stalin had been in sole command in Russia now for ten years: he had killed off everyone who might be a rival – all Trotsky's followers inside Russia and all the old-guard Bolsheviks who had once been their joint colleagues – everyone of any importance, that is, except Trotsky, whom presumably he had not felt confident enough to have had killed when he had exiled him in 1929. But now Trotsky was cut off in Mexico: certainly Stalin was in a strong enough position to have his last and greatest rival killed; there was hardly enough feeling left in the Communist world to be stimulated by Trotsky as a martyr. But for this reason, too, there should have been little sense in killing him. But there had been little sense of this sort in communist politics for the last ten years.

31

Trotsky had been made by Stalin a scapegoat for all the disasters in Russia, which were considerable. Stalin needed a scapegoat because according to Communist theory there should not have been any disasters – Communist theory was supposed to be "scientific" and with the establishment of the workers' state disasters in agriculture and industry should not come from within but only from without. The failure of a wheatcrop, for instance, could not easily be explained by natural causes – this would in some way be a betrayal of principle – but it could be explained by the agency of saboteurs, because they were outside the system. But saboteurs had to have had some contact with the system in order to be effective in their mythical role as scapegoats. Trotsky, to Stalin, had become the arch-saboteur; he and his agents were held to be responsible not only for industrial breakdown but for such things as the way in which trains on the Russian railways did not run on time and epidemics of swine-fever among pigs. These occurrences in Russia were supposed to have been organised by Trotsky in Western Europe or Mexico. In the light of Trotsky's powerlessness and solitude this sort of belief would seem to depend on a respect more for magic than for science; and the whole atmosphere of the Moscow purges and trials of the 1930's does appear to be shot through with nightmare fantasies and projections. But the story of this comes later.

In 1940 Stalin did wish implacably to kill Trotsky, and he had the means to do it with the enormous apparatus of his secret police. By this time Trotsky was not even needed as scapegoat: with the war there had come other external villains for Stalin to project his nightmare failures on to. While he was in league with the Nazis he could project all evil on to capitalist England and America, and when he was in league with England and America he could project it on to the Nazis.

Trotsky knew that Stalin would try to kill him: he might have been flattered that his power was still so mythical. There were hundreds of thousands of Communists all over the world who in fact did believe Stalin's propaganda that Trotsky was the arch-enemy of the Soviet State; that he was a conspirator in the pay of imperialists and fascists; that he not only destroyed factories but put nails in butter. People who could believe that leaders of the Russian Revolution had almost from the beginning been working to destroy the Revolution – which was what the Moscow trials set out to prove – could believe, presumably, anything: it was not difficult for them to see Trotsky, the chief leader of the Revolution, as the leader of the saboteurs against it. With the advent of the materialist workers' state it seemed that the minds of its inhabitants had become very largely a prey to fantasy. Trotsky saw this – with his usual irony. It seemed that after the death of belief, as in its life, men were still being asked to demonstrate their allegiance by an acceptance of absurdity.

And there were enough young men at the time – too young to remember when Trotsky was Lenin's right-hand man and at the centre of Soviet power – who still needed a scapegoat for the failures of left-wing politics outside Russia; above all, for the disasters of the Spanish Civil War. There Communist intervention had been far less effective than that of Mussolini or Hitler: in the light of later evidence it seems that Stalin himself withheld support for the Republicans since he did not want to cause too much trouble: at the time, to left-wing devotees, this seemed incredible, and blame was put upon the split between the orthodox Communists and left-wing anarchists – and thus upon Trotsky. The anarchists were not even organised Trotskyites but had been influenced by Trotsky's ideas. But they did not co-operate with the Stalinists. And then as so often within the party – as in Brussels in 1903 and in the subsequent struggles between Bolsheviks and Mensheviks – the opposing factions spent almost as much energy attacking each other as attacking their enemies. After their defeat, a lot of young men who had fought in the Republican Army had left Spain and had taken refuge wherever possible; many had come to Mexico, which had been the only country to send an official contingent to fight on the Republican side. These veterans in 1940 needed a victim on which to vent a bitterness even beyond that of politics – of their personal shame and betrayal.

From the time of his arrival in Mexico Trotsky had been attacked violently by the Communist press. *La Voz de Mexico*, *El Popular*, and *Futuro* had protested against President Cardenas' granting him asylum; they continued to call for his expulsion. This campaign increased in virulence during the early months of 1940; it was conducted in the usual slanging-match style – "Trotsky, the old traitor, demonstrates to us that the older he grows the more cur-like he becomes . . ." "What a slippery fish is the little old traitor!" ". . . the new pontiff, Leon XXX, in view of the thirty pieces of silver of the dirtied Judas . . .". As Trotsky himself remarked – "This is the way people write who are preparing to change the pen for the machine gun." On May-day 1940, 20,000 uniformed Communists marched through Mexico City, some with banners which said "Out with Trotsky!" Trotsky knew that so long as President Cardenas stood firm about allowing him to remain in Mexico then sooner or later an attempt on his life would be made. This was "logical". The attempt would be made either by trained agents of Stalin's secret political police – the G.P.U. – who were rumoured now to be arriving in force in Mexico City, by the disgruntled veterans from Spain, by distraught members of the Mexican Communist Party, or by some combination of all three. Also supposedly out to destroy Trotsky at this time were the Nazi Gestapo, now working with the G.P.U.; also, just conceivably, American agents – because Trotskyites in America were causing trouble in the Unions. But this was almost certainly mythical.

Against this formidable array Trotsky built up his defences at Coyoacan and marshalled his own private army – his wife, his grandson, three servants and six secretaries or guards. There were also ten Mexican policemen in a hut outside the house who were kept on duty in two shifts; they were there for Trotsky's protection by order of President Cardenas. Trotsky's own guards inside the grounds had one machine gun in the watchtower and a variety of rifles and pistols. They were none of them used to firearms.

The story of the first assassination attempt – the raid of the 24th May – has become so befogged by self-justifications, dialectics, and the central mystery of the raid, that is easy to forget that the main events are not disputed – the fact that an armed gang of about twenty men broke into Trotsky's house at night and fired hundreds of bullets into his bedroom. This, it would seem, was an occurrence striking enough to diminish argument; but Trotsky was someone who in any situation would look for a political advantage, and the participants in the raid were unusual.

The raid was organised and led by David Alfaro Siqueiros, the painter – who together with Rivera and Orozco had been a leader of the Mexican school of painting of the 1930's. This school was, and is, immensely exciting; it was in Mexico at this time that such painting and painters flourished – the painters believed that aesthetic creativity could not be separated from political passion; that art was both a reflection of, and a means of transforming, society. They painted for the most part huge murals in public buildings depicting the history, the violence and the mythology of the workers' struggle. The great Mexican painters of the 1930's and 40's were a renaissance type of man – they lived as fighters as well as artists – Rivera had founded the Mexican Communist party; Orozco was active in politics anarchically in his home province; Siqueiros was leader of the Mexican Mineworkers' Union and had been a Republican Colonel in the Spanish War. He, like Rivera, was a man of gigantic energy; he was more of a buccaneer and more constant. Rivera had befriended Trotsky against orthodox Communists: later, in order to reinstate himself with Stalinists, he was to claim he had only lured Trotsky to Mexico to betray him to his death. Siqueiros had taken Rivera's place as the effective figurehead of the Mexican Communist Party; during the time of the demonstrations against Trotsky he had assembled round him other left-wing painters and his friends from the Mineworker's Union. He continued painting – one of his most striking works at this time is the huge fresco "Portrait of the Bourgeoisie" on the staircase of the Mexican Electrician's Union building. The painting shows capitalist monsters with diabolical machinery; soldiers in gas-masks and their tortured victims; crowds marching blindly to war while a parrot orates into a microphone. Siqueiros became obsessed with the need to do something about the so-called arch-traitor, Trotsky.

The conspirators gathered in a studio-room in Cuba Street in the city on the night of 23rd–24th May. They were mostly artists, ex-soldiers, mineworkers, the unemployed. There was with them an agent of the G.P.U. known as Felipe. They had acquired police uniforms: they dressed up. The second-in-command of the raid, a painter called Pujol, wore the uniform of an army lieutenant: Siqueiros himself wore the uniform of a major, with dark glasses and a false moustache. They carried ropes, rope-ladders, rubber gloves, incendiary bombs, a rotary saw, several revolvers and at least two machine guns. There are stories that the moustache that Siqueiros wore was a "Hitler" moustache; that instead of an officers' hat he had a first-war "Kaiser" helmet. This is not unlikely. To a great Communist artist, as to his intended victim, the conjunction of murderous solemnity and farce might seem a part of dialectics.

Chapter 4

Trotsky's home at Coyoacan is in the shape of a "T": the top forms one of the outside walls of the rectangular enclosure and the stem juts out into the garden. Along the top of the "T" are the library, the dining-room and the kitchen: in the stem were Trotsky's study, Trotsky's and Natalya's bedroom, and at the end Seva's bedroom. All the building was on one floor, except in the corner above the kitchen where there was a two-storied tower. The guards lived and slept in a line of outhouses along the wall at the back of the garden.

Outside in the Avenue Viena was the police post with five policemen permanently on duty. One of the preliminary moves of the raiders was to find out about the movements of the policemen and to try to ensure that on the night they would be distracted. Two girls, Julia and Anita, had been set up in a house opposite and posed as prostitutes. These girls not only observed the comings and goings of the police but succeeded in seducing at least one of them. On the night of the raid the girls gave a party. The police were invited. Julia and Anita turned out later to be the ex-wife and the girl-friend of two of the raiders – Serrano Andonegui and Mariano Vasquez.

The twenty raiders piled into four cars in the city and drove out to Coyoacan. They laughed and joked on the way: they were given detailed instruction. A few more men joined them in a street near the Avenue Viena. Their first task was to overcome what they hoped were the already softened-up policemen. It was about four o'clock in the morning. One party of raiders – dressed as policemen – moved to the police-post and had little difficulty in disarming and in tying up those still on duty. Another group moved to the outside door of Trotsky's house. This door led into a garage from which an inner doorway led into the garden. The outer door was always locked and guarded. When the raiders arrived however it was immediately opened. The guard on duty was Robert Sheldon Harte, a young American. He had come from New York and had been six weeks with Trotsky.

There is still uncertainty about why Sheldon Harte opened the door. Trotskyites like to make out that he was loyal to Trotsky; that he was taken in either by some familiar face amongst the raiders or by the fact that the raiders were dressed as policemen – it was the policy of Trotsky's household to be friendly to the police. But there were strict orders that no one was to be admitted at night.

The minor members of Trotsky's entourage changed frequently. They were mostly provided, and paid for, by sympathisers in America. They were young men who had a few months to spare between colleges or jobs; left-wing devotees eager to travel or to spend time at the feet of the Master. Trotsky welcomed new faces if they were serious; he liked a fresh audience on which to practice his arts of rhetoric and persuasion. Sheldon Harte had been well known amongst Trotskyites in New York, but there could not always be a complete check on the credentials of a newcomer. Trotsky himself to the end of his life protested his faith in Sheldon's loyalty; but he also wrote after the raid that "the possibility of a G.P.U. agent managing to become even one of my guards cannot be excluded from consideration".

Sheldon Harte opened the door. The raiders moved through the garage and into the garden. The rooms in the stem of the "T" which projected into the garden all had french windows and connecting doors between the rooms. The raiders split into four groups; one went to the window of Seva's bedroom at the end of the "T", one to the window of Trotsky's and Natalya's bedroom in the middle, one through the dining-room and Trotsky's study to the connecting door between it and Trotsky's bedroom, and the fourth to the back, where there was a space between the stem of the "T" and the outbuildings where the guards slept. No one tried to prevent them. Everyone seemed to be asleep. Siqueiros himself went to the back with his machine-gun; his task was to prevent the guards from leaving their quarters. The raiders were now on all four sides of Trotsky's bedroom. They opened fire through windows and doors into the bedroom simultaneously. This, at least, was the story of their intended victims. It was surprising that the raiders did not shoot each other down. The firing, Trotsky said, went on for "three to five minutes". It sounded as if there were two or three machine guns. None of the guards appeared to fire back. One guard said later that he had "levelled his gun at one of the assailants, drawn back the hammer, and then torn by indecision lowered his weapon". Trotsky had taken sleeping powders that night: at first he thought the gunfire was fireworks. Then Natalya pulled him "very, very gently" off the bed with her and on to the floor between the bed and the wall. There they lay, while "the shooting continued incessantly". Trotsky thought that two hundred shots had been fired of which "a hundred fell right here near us". Natalya tried to shield him with her body, but "by means of whispers and gestures I convinced her to lie flat on the floor". After the firing had stopped, Natalya remembered thinking – "Why does no one come? Why does no one call us?" She believed she saw, in the dark, illuminated by the flare of an incendiary bomb, "a silhouette; the curve of a helmet, shining buttons, an elongated face". This figure was later said – not by Natalya but by one of Trotsky's guards – to have walked into the bedroom and to have fired eight shots from his pistol at point-blank range into the beds. There is still one bullet-mark in the floor at the place above which the beds once were. Then the figure left. The raiders ran for the garage. They started up Trotsky's two cars – the keys were kept in them in case of emergency which the raiders seemed to know – and drove them into the street. The raiders piled in, taking Sheldon Harte with them. He was seen by the tied-up policemen to be led by the arm to the car but to climb in willingly. One policemen even said that Sheldon drove one of the cars. The cars went away. One was found later abandoned stuck in the mud not far from the house, the other was picked up in Mexico City.

Trotsky and Natalya heard Seva in the next room shouting "Grandfather!" They emerged from their corner at the side of the bed; Natalya pounded on the connecting doors which were riddled with bullet-holes and had jammed; the secretaries and guards at last came running. The raiders had left two incendiary bombs; one was setting fire to the grass on the lawn and the other was burning at the entrance to Seva's room. Natalya put this out with a rug, being burned herself on the arms and legs in the process. Seva had been wounded in the toe; he too had rolled on to the floor at the sound of firing and a bullet coming through his french window and aimed at the door of Trotsky's room had riccocheted and struck him. He ran out into the garden leaving a trail of blood. Trotsky thought that Seva had been kidnapped, and Seva remembers his grandfather dashing out into the garden and taking a pot-shot with his pistol at a figure on the canal-bank above the level of the wall at the back. This figure turned out to be that of an old woman. Trotsky missed. There was a third bomb, unexploded, in the garden, with enough dynamite in it to have blown up the house.

By the time the Chief of Police arrived all the occupants of the house seemed extraordinarily calm. They had put out the fires and were tidying the damage. The guards answered questions about what had happened in cheerful and even condescending monosyllables. Seva was playing quietly in the garden where the grass was still smouldering from the incendiary bomb. Trotsky made his statement to the police in which he said that he and Natalya had been sleeping when they had heard the sound of gunfire and then they had rolled to the floor. The firing had come from all four sides; by a "happy accident" the bullets had all passed above them. It was also possible, Trotsky said, that "my wife and I came to the aid of the happy accident by not losing our heads, not flying around the room, not crying out or calling for help when it was useless to do so, not shouting when it was senseless, but remained quietly on the floor pretending to be dead". The incendiary bombs had been placed to destroy his archives, he said, to succeed in which would be as important to Stalin and the G.P.U. as his death.

Colonel Salazar, Chief of the Mexican Secret Police, was convinced that Trotsky's story was untrue – either the entire raiding party was a fake and had been staged by Trotsky himself in order to gain public sympathy and to discredit his opponents, or possibly the raid itself was genuine but Trotsky had been tipped off and had been hiding in another part of the house. The reasons for Salazar's conviction were Trotsky's almost miraculous escape, the extraordinary behaviour of the guards in not firing a shot in his defence, the amazing mixture of efficiency and incompetence apparently shown by the raiders, and the calm and conspiratorial atmosphere in the house afterwards. It was also true that Trotsky would gain sympathy from such a raid, and his opponents in the Mexican Communist Party would be looked on with opprobrium and might even be arrested – which in fact was what happened.

The continuing attitudes of Trotsky and his guards did little to dispel Salazar's suspicions. Otto Schuessler, one of Trotsky's secretaries, explained that he had been taken by surprise by the raiders and his machine-gun had jammed so he had remained in the guardhouse. Charles Cornell, another guard, said he had fired one shot at an unidentified figure running across the court-yard but had missed and then had done nothing. Trotsky did not seem perturbed. The cook said she had seen Otto standing carrying a pistol during the raid watchfully and passively in the kitchen doorway. The parlourmaid said there had been long and secret consultations between Trotsky and his guards on the evening before the attack. There were slight discrepancies in the various stories – Natalya said she had stood up and walked across the bedroom after the firing through the windows and doors and she had seen firing still continuing from a eucalyptus tree in the garden: Trotsky said they had remained on the floor till all the raiders had gone. Joseph Hansen, a secretary, told the story of the man coming into the bedroom and firing eight shots: Trotsky and Natalya, by the beds, had not seen him: but, as Trotsky said, "an analysis of the trajectory of the bullets proved irrefutably that eight shots . . . could have been fired only inside the bedroom itself". Trotsky, when asked by Salazar whom he thought was responsible for the raid, took Salazar by the arm and led him to one side in the garden and then whispered dramatically "Joseph Stalin!" Salazar said he was "stupefied" by this. It seemed to confirm his conviction that the raid was faked, and he decided to take into custody for questioning two of Trotsky's guards and his servants.

Salazar had counted seventy-three bullet holes above and around the beds: some of the bullet holes are still there as a memorial. But Salazar thought that if the raiders were genuine they would be working in with the G.P.U.: it continued to seem inconceivable that agents trained for murder could fire with machine-guns into Trotsky's bedroom for "three to five minutes" and, simply, miss. And it seemed just as odd that Trotsky should take this for granted. But Salazar was not trained in dialectics. Trotsky himself paid a tribute to the "high technological level of the attempt", but again put the failure down to "accident, which is an inevitable element in every war".

It is not Trotsky's friends but his enemies who still like to claim that the story of the raid was faked – that Trotsky had been tipped off and was not in the bedroom. For them it is more important that he should be made to seem dishonest than that he should seem clever. Also this excuses something of the incompetence of the raiders if not their failure. Trotsky continued to stick to his story that he was of course as he had said in his bedroom: his friends are still adamant that he could not have told a lie: they too want to insist that he was honest rather than that he could have been a trickster. But the key witness here is Seva: he says with certainty that if his grandfather had been hiding in another room it is impossible that he would have left himself, Seva, exposed in the bedroom. Seva as a witness carried conviction. So Trotsky's story is accepted. Seva still lives in his grandfather's old house, where not only the bullet holes in the walls but the rooms where Trotsky lived and worked are kept as a memorial.

And the oddities in the story could in fact be explained, as Trotsky said, in terms of the accidents of war – the ways in which firing a machine-gun from the hip does spray the bullets upwards; not so many rounds are usually fired as are imagined; it is easy to miss one's aim in the dark; memories do get fanciful at moments of fright and danger; even staunch political acolytes can become paralysed in the presence of machine-guns. It seems likely that the raiders did roughly as was claimed but were just incompetent; it is not a guarantee of efficiency to have been a veteran of the Spanish Civil War. And perhaps there was some protective halo around the magic name of Trotsky. It is one thing to talk of killing; another to shoot deliberately at one's sleeping great enemy in the dark. The raiders might simply have been frightened – even of shooting one another. There remained however the mystery of Sheldon Harte, and of Trotsky's insistence on his loyalty.

It had been established that Sheldon had let the raiders in: then he had been seen driving off with them, at least without a struggle. After this there was no news of him. Sheldon's father, when he arrived in Mexico from New York to look for his son, said that he had had no idea that Sheldon had been working for Trotsky: in his bedroom at home he had had a photograph of Stalin. Evidence turned up years later from someone who claimed to have been his girl-friend at the time that Sheldon was in fact a Communist who sympathised with Stalin – not perhaps a trained agent of the G.P.U. but certainly someone who went to Trotsky's household as a spy and probably a traitor. But on the other hand Natalya at the time would not hear of anything like this. She wrote – "poor boy . . . what has happened to our friend,

43

our guard?" and reminisced – "Sheldon loved to take walks. In his free hours he took walks around the environs of Coyoacan and brought back bouquets of field flowers!" And Trotsky himself, protesting Sheldon's innocence, seemed swayed by more than just a desire to make excuses for his own misjudgment or not to embarrass the friends who had sent Sheldon to him from New York. Trotsky probably had a passionate need to believe in people's loyalty; this was the one power of which he had not been deprived.

It seems likely now, according to what is known of the passions or lack of passions of the time, that Sheldon might not have belonged wholeheartedly to either the Trotskyites or to the faction that wanted to kill him: like so many young men at the end of the 1930's he was most probably a mixed-up college boy with a social conscience who was torn between orthodox Communism and Trotsky's ideas; he might or might not have been approached by an agent of the G.P.U. in New York, but even if he had been such an approach might have seemed, as it often did, civilised and charming; he might have gone to Mexico to find out something about himself as much as to spy. And once he was there, he could have fallen under the spell of the Old Man's charm and felt some genuine loyalty. But then he would not have known where he was: the G.P.U., if they had once touched him, would not have let him go. So he would have become uncertain whether Trotsky was the defender of the true workers' Utopia or the betrayer of an actual socialist state – he would have gone from side to side in his head like a ping-pong ball, as so many young men did at the time. And when he opened the door into Trotsky's house he might not have quite known what he was up to; he might have been betraying Trotsky or he might have been under the impression that he had given some warning to Trotsky; which perhaps he even had. One of the fantasies of politicians is that men act according to reason and not by compulsions; but compulsions are often arbitrary when the pressures of opposites become intolerable. Trotsky could have recognised

44

this with his irony – but it was not in his interests to do so at the moment. Sheldon Harte was missing: he had been one of Trotsky's small band. Whatever Sheldon's motives, or lack of them, it seemed likely that he might become the victim of the violence of a hostile gang. And Trotsky, emotionally, was on the side of victims – when they were on the side of history or himself.

Chapter 5

When Colonel Salazar took two of Trotsky's guards and his servants off for questioning Trotsky was left more defenceless than ever – and he was sure that after the failure of the first attempt a second would come soon. He wrote to President Cardenas complaining that not only had he been attacked with machine guns by a gang of local Stalinists while the police who were supposed to be guarding him had not fired a shot, but these same police were now depriving him of his own guards. President Cardenas saw the logic of this, and ordered Salazar to release Trotsky's men and to look for the real culprits. Salazar did so, at first relucantly.

This was the beginning of Trotsky's strenuous efforts to justify himself and his guards in the matter of the first assassination attempt and to persuade the police and the public that the raid had been carried out by Stalinists. He went to enormous lengths in this – peppering the police and the press with letters and advice. The press had picked up the story that the raid might have been a fake: they noted the slight discrepancies in Trotsky's and his household's stories: Trotsky railed against the "absurd idea of self-assault". "What aim could I pursue in venturing on so monstrous, repugnant and dangerous an enterprise? It is hinted that I wanted to blacken Stalin and his G.P.U. But would another assault add anything at all to the reputation of a man who has destroyed an entire old generation of the Bolshevik party? It is said that I wanted to create difficulties for the Mexican government; what possible motives could I have for creating difficulties for the only government that has been hospitable to me?" About the discrepancies – "If a man living in *émigré* solitude proved capable of mobilizing twenty conspirators and obtaining for them police uniforms and machine guns then he ought to be capable of preparing an answer as to his whereabouts at the time of the assault." But Trotsky was less convincing in the matter of Sheldon Harte. He argued that if Sheldon had been an agent of the G.P.U. he could have stabbed Trotsky quietly any time in the past six weeks. But the G.P.U., for psychological or practical reasons, often went to devious lengths to obscure its traces: it was necessary for secret political work to be bewildering to remain secret.

Salazar had assumed men acted rationally: this was a basic assumption of detective work as well as of politics. But as soon as he turned his attention from Trotsky's entourage and looked for clues amongst members of the Mexican Communist party he found, as Trotsky had said he would, a trail of evidence that led quickly to the raid's actual leaders – Siqueiros, Pujol, Serrano Andonegui. Trotsky had even suggested that he look for Siqueiros. Siqueiros himself was in hiding: but Andonegui was arrested.

Andonegui was a member of the Political Bureau of the Mexican Communist Party and had been trained, Trotsky claimed, in G.P.U. work in Moscow and Spain. The facts came out about the acquisition and distribution of guns and uniforms: the house was discovered where the two pseudo-prostitutes had carried out their diversions. It was found that one of the girls, Julia, was the ex-wife of Andonegui. Even the mysterious "Felipe" was traced – the police arrived at his lodgings and saw him driving away in an American car. They did not recognise him at the time, but in his room, among other clues, they found some "underwear bought on the Boulevard Saint Michel". From this Salazar concluded that "without a doubt he had come from Moscow via Paris, under orders to prepare the assassination of Trotsky". Police enquiries were back to normal.

The lover of the second pseudo-prostitute, Anita, was picked up and told his story. He was an out-of-work electrician called

Vasquez. He and Anita and Julia, he said, had all been working for Siqueiros. He had been installed in a house near that of the others in Coyoacan: he had been paid by Siqueiros at the rate of ten pesos a day. In the middle of May, shortly before the raid, he had been picked up in a car by Siqueiros and Siqueiros's wife Angelica Arenal and they had all driven into the town to buy a folding bed and materials for painting. Then they had gone some thirteen miles out of the city to an empty part of the country called The Desert of the Lions. There Vasquez and Angelica Arenal had carried the bed and the painting materials a mile from the road up a hill to a dilapidated farmhouse. Vasquez had been told to stay there. Angelica Arenal and Siqueiros had returned to the town.

Also staying in the house, Vasquez said, had been Luis Arenal, Angelica's brother, and two other colleagues of Siqueiros'. They had all stayed a week, doing nothing and receiving their wages. Then on the afternoon of May 23rd Vasquez had decided to go into the town and get drunk. When he had returned to the farmhouse the next day he found, from one of the conspirators left behind, that the job for which he had been hired but about which he had not known had taken place without him during the night. Pujol had come and collected Luis Arenal and one other conspirator: they had not returned: the man left behind had been told of the raid on Trotsky but not of the outcome.

On the evening of the 24th Luis Arenal had returned, Vasquez said, and had brought with him a young American with red hair. The two had seemed on friendly terms. Vasquez had been told that the young American was to stay in the farmhouse: Vasquez was to keep an eye on him, but the American could go out walking alone. Then Luis Arenal and the other two conspirators had left. Vasquez and the young American had stayed in the farmhouse on their own for several days: then Vasquez had got bored again and had picked up a drinking companion in the village. They had all three been at the farmhouse one day drinking when Luis Arenal had arrived back unexpectedly with his brother

48

Leopoldo. The brothers had seemed annoyed at the presence of a stranger; they had ordered him out; then they had chatted amicably for a time with the young American. They had spoken in English, which Vasquez did not understand. Then they had told Vasquez to go and not to come back. He had left them in the farmhouse with the American.

When Vasquez was picked up later by the police – during a routine check he was found wandering idly round the tenement where his parents lived – he told them of the journey to the farm-house with the folding bed and the painting materials but not, at first, of his further experiences there. The police, again as a check, went off to The Desert of the Lions in the middle of the night and climbed up the hill to the farmhouse, which was empty. There were three rooms with wooden floors beneath which was a basement where the ground sloped away at the back. In one of the rooms was a table with newspapers spread out at pages telling of the attack on Trotsky; in another the folding bed with a mattress that appeared to have been slashed at the head. The floor was covered with powdered lime. In the third room was an easel with an empty canvas. On the floors of all the rooms were the butts of hundreds of American cigarettes, and one or two spent cartridges.

When the police went to the basement they found a kitchen with an earthen floor and some of the earth disturbed. It was scattered with lime. The police had brought no digging equipment so they sent out for a peasant with a pickaxe. The peasant came and began digging. They worked in the light from their pocket torches.

After a time there was a smell; the pickaxe disclosed what Salazar said "resembled a human stomach". "There is no doubt," Salazar remembered thinking, "about its being a dead body!" He told the peasant who had been digging "Do not continue my good man!" and went off to find the local magistrate. He returned, during a wild rain storm and still in the night, with the magistrate, the Public Prosecutor, and a team of firemen with gas-masks.

The digging continued. The body was brought up. It appeared to be that of a giant, and made of copper. The action of the lime had made the skin turn red. Salazar cut off a lock of hair and washed it: it remained red. Sheldon Harte had had red hair. He had been very tall. The face was almost unrecognisable. The head had had a bullet through it, fired at close range. This was a usual method of execution of the G.P.U. It seemed that the victim might have been asleep on the bed upstairs: the lime on the floor had covered blood. There were bits of clothing half burned on a bonfire a few yards away.

Salazar went off to tell Trotsky. Trotsky was asleep and could not be woken, having taken his usual sleeping powders. Otto Schuessler went with Salazar to identify the body. He confirmed it was that of Sheldon. Sheldon's corpse was put on a stretcher and the cortege moved back down the hill. They had now been joined by a crowd of journalists, slithering and tumbling in the rain.

Trotsky made his appearance at the local police station the next morning. A small crowd had collected – whenever he went out a crowd seemed to collect – there was a stir, and the murmurs of "Trotsky! Trotsky!" He looked down at Sheldon's body. His eyes filled with tears.

Trotsky used Sheldon's murder as a proof for his insistence that Sheldon could not have been a traitor. He wrote – "Bob perished because he placed himself in the road of the assassins. He died for the ideas in which he believed. His memory is spotless." Trotsky named seven others of his aides or secretaries who had been murdered in various countries. "I leave aside the members of my family, two daughters and two sons, brought to their death by the G.P.U."

But there was still the evidence that Sheldon had seemed to go with the raiders willingly; evidence from an independent witness who had seen Sheldon going for walks from the farmhouse on his own without a guard. To this Trotsky did not listen. He did not want to.

50

Sheldon was perhaps murdered just because, as before, he could not make up his mind one way or the other. He had come from New York to spy on Trotsky and then probably had come under Trotsky's influence: it was too late not to let the raiders in but afterward he might have had doubts about what he had done. This would have been noticed. And the G.P.U. in any event was accustomed to getting rid of those who had worked for it after their job was done. In this way, there were no further betrayals.

Trotsky knew the methods of the G.P.U. His insistence on the innocence of Sheldon proved nothing except his own need of loyalty; possibly some sorrow that he had not managed to influence Sheldon as he had tried to do. It would have been sad for him to have to admit that a young man whom he and Natalya had trusted and whom he had had time to impress with his arguments and his personality had been unimpressed to the point of being an accomplice in his attempted murder. He always trusted Natalya's opinion about people. And when Trotsky chose to believe something – whether as a matter of policy or emotion – he did not change: and he wanted the world to know of his belief. He had a stone plaque put upon the wall of the garden near the garage through which the raiders had got in. The plaque said *In Memory of Robert Sheldon Harte, 1915–1940. Murdered by Stalin.*

Trotsky had defeated the perpetrators of the raid: by the "happy accident" of their incompetence and at the cost of Sheldon he had in fact gained public sympathy and the leaders of the Mexican Communist Party were in hiding or under arrest or in disarray. But the raiders had still won some psychological victory. For months Trotsky was taken up with justifying himself and stating the case against his attackers in the public controversy about the raid and the murder; he gave up his "real work" which was the biography of Stalin and his projected book on Lenin in order to refute, in Natalya's words, "lies" which were "self-evident". His opponents were even suggesting that Sheldon might have been murdered by Trotskyites in order to try to disprove the story of "self-assault". It was then that Natalya remembered Trotsky growing tired. "He slept poorly, dozing off and waking up in the self-same thoughts." Then – "A feeling of the greatest alarm would seize me." From this time on Trotsky never seriously got down to his real work again. His language often became petty in the old slanging-match style that in the past in periods of exhaustion had bedevilled him. It was as if he had been infected by the virus of his enemies. He might have felt some genuine futility in the wild arguments about the raid and the death of Sheldon; but this could not be admitted. To the world he had to say that his concern was only in "elucidating the logic of facts". He added with his usual undertone of prophesy but in reverse – "against this logic the falsifiers will break their skulls".

Chapter 6

The epilogue to the first assassination attempt and the murder of Sheldon took place after Trotsky's death and in a sense was swamped by this: but the story retained its flavour of grisliness tinged with farce. During the summer most of the members of the Mexican Communist Party involved in the raid had been arrested, but the leaders – Siqueiros, Pujol, the Arenal brothers and the mysterious Felipe – remained at large. Felipe was thought to have got out of the country and in this guise at least does not turn up in the story again: by later investigators he was rumoured to have been spotted in various places and at various times in the form of a spy called George Mink, an ex-ambassador called Haikis, or a top official of the G.P.U. called Leonid Eitigon. The latter was also rumoured to materialise from time to time as Sakhov, Valery, Comrade Pablo or General Kotov. In the Secret Service world it is an advantage to be disintegrated. Trotsky might have had memories of this from the old days when he himself had been Antid Oto, Pero, Petr Petrovitch – or Bronstein.

The Arenal brothers fled to New York. They did not come back to Mexico until after the actual assassination. Then, in an atmosphere of anti-climax, the charges brought against them concerning the raid were largely dropped. Charges of conspiring against the life of Trotsky were dropped because under Mexican law conspiracy must be that of planning to commit crimes in "general terms" and not against a particular individual or family: and charges of impersonating public officials were dropped because although it was undeniable that the raiders had dressed up as policemen yet they had not "usurped the function of policemen" – that is, they had been attacking Trotsky. This was a fine area for Marxist logic.

Charges concerning the murder of Sheldon were dropped because although there was evidence that Sheldon had been taken to the farmhouse by one of the Arenal brothers and had last been seen with the two of them, after which he had been found shot and the Arenal brothers had fled to New York, all this did not provide a *prima facie* case for murder because, as the Arenals' lawyer said – "Harte could have been killed by a fifth column organisation organised by Trotsky." Trotsky himself when still alive had foreseen this line of defence: he had written "It will appear that the G.P.U. desires to convince humanity that David Alfaro Siqueiros is my agent, and that by my initiative he organised the assault. ... Will not the G.P.U. demand of Siqueiros, under pain of death, that tomorrow he declares himself to have been secretly a Trotskyist? Will not Siqueiros declare that he killed Bob Harte in the course of a 'self-assault'?" This was shortly after the time of the Moscow trials, when politicians had become accustomed to the experience that the more absurd the lie, the more likely committed devotees were to have to believe it.

Siqueiros had gone into hiding, and the police received no information about him except in the form, perhaps not surprisingly, of long letters addressed to them from both himself and Trotsky. Siqueiros wrote saying that he would present himself to the police at any time that he was required; they replied that he was required, and he didn't present himself. He also wrote letters to the press in Mexico City attacking President Cardenas for his continued protection of Trotsky and criticising the police for the "unbridled violence" of their pursuit of the perpetrators of the assassination attempt.

Trotsky wrote saying that he had reliable information that Siqueiros was about to set sail from the port of Manzanillo on a boat taking a cargo of iron to Japan: the police sent a detachment to Manzanillo and inspected all the boats but did not find

Siqueiros. After this the efforts of the police slackened because they were occupied in keeping order during a presidential election. Then in September Salazar received a clue that a woman who looked like Siqueiros's wife Angelica Arenal had been seen travelling by train to Guadalajara – "fairly tall, rather broad, with an oval face, wide brow, straight nose, large mouth, thin lips and medium complexion". Salazar was off in pursuit: it was known Siqueiros had friends in the area. Salazar disguised two of his aides as salesmen – one travelling in ornamental plants and the other in crazy paving. Salazar himself let his beard grow and disguised himself as a "political propagandist". There were still parliamentary elections in the area. Salazar even went to the length of hiring a sham parliamentary candidate so that he could tour the countryside without suspicion with a lorry-load of thirty soldiers and a pile of electoral tracts.

Siqueiros's friends were miners whom he had helped to organise in a strike in 1926. They were centred round the town of Hostotipaquillo. The political propagandist and the parliamentary candidate and the thirty soldiers and the two travelling salesmen arrived in the town and went to see the Mayor: he too was said to be a friend of Siqueiros. In spite of Salazar's beard the Mayor immediately recognised him. (All this is described in dashing style in Salazar's book *Murder in Mexico*: the conversation went – " 'Come, come, Colonel: you are the Chief of Secret Police in Mexico!' 'I assure you that you are mistaken,' I replied, getting annoyed.") The Mayor also almost immediately agreed to betray Siqueiros: he admitted that Siqueiros was hiding in the district and that he was under the protection of "The Municipal Chairman, his secretary, the second-in-command of the 1st Squadron of the 58th Reserve Corps, and the local Chief of Police". At the moment he was in the mountains, taking the air.

Salazar set off for the nearest mountain. Night overtook him, and he had to turn back. After three days of this to-and-fro he came across an old miner who was a friend of Siqueiros's and who had worked with him during the 1926 strike. The miner almost immediately agreed to talk. Siqueiros was hiding in a farmhouse, the miner said; he was looked after by the family and was guarded by a gunman called, oddly, Orozco. He was sleeping in some stables, and was visited occasionally by his wife Angelica and his brother who was called Jesus.

Salazar approached the farmhouse with great care and surrounded it with his thirty soldiers and his parliamentary candidate and his travelling salesmen and they all attacked at dawn. They found the gunman called Orozco wandering in the woods with a .22 rifle, and a family in the farmhouse too frightened to speak. Siqueiros was outside lying on a mattress by a stream. The meeting, in Salazar's description, went – " 'Good morning!' we both said at the same time: 'Hullo what are you doing here?' I added in a serious tone." On their way back to Mexico City the two chatted amicably about their experiences in war. On the road they were met by a welcoming party of government officials and hundreds of journalists. There were speeches. The political candidate had begun to take his role seriously, and decided to stay and carry it on in the area.

Months later Siqueiros was charged as the Arenal brothers had been with planning the May raid on Trotsky. In a preliminary examination Siqueiros claimed that the object of the raid had been not to kill Trotsky but just to frighten him – to draw public attention to the contradictory attitudes of President Cardenas in granting Trotsky asylum while professing to remain friendly to the Soviet Union. The raiders had also possibly wanted to destroy or to carry off his archives. And Trotsky was, in fact, still alive. The judge was impressed by the argument that twenty trained men with machine guns could hardly be so incompetent as not to be able to kill an unarmed man in his bed if they had truly wanted to; but he was still perplexed. Did it really require several hundred bullets and two incendiary bombs in a bedroom, he asked, to frighten someone and to carry off their documents? Siqueiros replied in fine political style – "Without referring to the concrete action of May 24th but to the hypothesis or logic that your question presupposes, I feel compelled to say that the number of shots that are necessary depends on the physical defensive means at the disposal of the person whose documents you want to carry off."

The same style was adopted by the defendants in an investigation into the death of Sheldon Harte. When asked a direct question about the murder, Siqueiros replied – "Without knowledge of the circumstances in which this happened I cannot venture a judgment on the matter, in as much as repressions of a political type are linked to specific attitudes of the victims and these specific attitudes are unknown to me at the moment." The charges against Siqueiros concerning Sheldon, as those against the Arenal brothers, were dropped; it was held that Sheldon could have been murdered not only by a fifth column organised by Trotsky, but simply for robbery.

During most of the examinations Siqueiros blew smoke-screens around the awkward questions and did not care about contradictions or simply answered that he did not know. There was one moment during his personal statement about the attempt on Trotsky however when he seemed to speak, though still with difficulty, of his own feelings: of – "another hypothesis that nobody can dare exclude; that is, the hypothesis of the independent act, the autonomous action, an action conceived, organised and applied by those people who are in no way linked to national or international organisations. Who would dare to say that Trotsky was hated only by Stalin? Trotsky was hated by millions of every nationality, all over the world, who were convinced of his traitor's role through the dialectics of communism."

But the political prevarications were usually in control. A classic statement of this kind was that of Andonegui – an experienced member of the Political Bureau of the Mexican Communist Party. When asked the question had he, or had he not, tried to kill Trotsky, he replied – "Trotsky is a counter-revolutionary and an enemy of the working class. Were he to die, or be killed, I would personally be pleased. That doesn't mean I would kill him or cause him to be killed. The Mexican Communist party does not give orders for people to be killed. Trotsky is a political, not a personal, enemy. We follow the Leninist doctrine against acts of personal terrorism. However, if the evidence you have before you is true – if indeed I did help in preparation for the raid on Trotsky – then you have every right to make the logical assumption that I might have been implicated in the assassination attempt."

Only minor charges against Siqueiros and the others remained – those of damage to property and the theft of two cars. Soviet Russia was fighting Nazi Germany by this time, and Trotsky was long since dead. The Mexican government wanted to stay friendly with the Soviet Union – and thus with local Communists. These latter were now backing Siqueiros, which they had not always done. Just after the May 24th attempt, when it seemed likely that the major charges against Siqueiros would be taken up, the Communist hierarchy had tried to disown him: they had referred to him as an "uncontrolled element considered half mad". But by 1942 he was back as a hero. The Party in the war had become used to these sudden changes. Diego Rivera, who had been Trotsky's great ally and instrumental in bringing him to Mexico, was now claiming he had only done this to lure him to his death.

Siqueiros was let out on bail. Petitions were sent to President Cardenas by "independent intellectuals" arguing that "artists and men of science" were the "bulwarks of culture and progress". Through the agency of Pablo Neruda, the communist poet, Siqueiros was allowed to jump bail and go to Chile, where he settled for a time. His wife Angelica Arenal and their children had gone to Russia. In Chile Siqueiros got on with his marvellous paintings.

Siqueiros was a visionary and an adventurer and in his own field something of a revolutionary genius in the way that Trotsky was in his. For once Trotsky had seemed to have a fittingly paradoxical opponent. The two men were alike in the scope of their concern and in the forcefulness of their energy. Siqueiros, like Trotsky, had been in and out of prison several times; he said he had been in front of firing squads and only at the last moment reprieved; his artistic work was inextricably involved with his political. In 1940, at the time of the raid, he was working on the enormous mural "Portrait of the Bourgeoisie". This was the painting of which a central figure is a monstrous parrot orating into a microphone. His fellow workers on this were the painters Antonio Pujol and Luis Arenal – who also played leading parts in the raid on Trotsky. Siqueiros had written – "Let us work on the most conspicuous walls of tall modern buildings, on the most strategically situated emplacements in the workers' suburbs, in trade-union offices, in public squares, in sport stadiums and in open-air theatres." Also – "When class oppression by the ruling class comes to an end painting will be a genuinely pure art, completely free from any decorative, anecdotal, descriptive of imitative intention . . . an art born solely of the immense joy derived from the interplay of textures, forms, volumes, colours and rhythms".

Trotsky would have agreed with this. He himself was writing about art at much the same time – "The style of official Soviet painting is being described as 'Socialist realism' . . . The realism consists in imitating provincial daguerreotype pictures of the third quarter of the previous century; the socialist style in using tricks of affected photography to represent events that have never taken place . . . But there is always implied, conscious or un-conscious, active or passive, optimistic or pessimistic, a protest against reality in any (genuine) artistic creation . . . Truly intellectual creation is incompatible with lies, hypocrisy, and the spirit of conformity . . . Artistic creation has its laws . . . Art can be the revolution's great ally only in so far as it remains true to itself."

Siqueiros's revolutionary innovations were in matters of technique. He used spray-guns, chemical paints, metal sheets hammered into relief: his frescos plunge round the corners of rooms and embody doors and windows. Trotsky did not talk of Siqueiros's revolution. Siqueiros did not stand back from history far enough to see Trotsky's.

Siqueiros is still (1971) working in the suburbs of Mexico City. He is constructing an enormous building of painted panels mounted on iron frames: the work depicts *The March of Humanity*. A dense multitude of anguished figures seems to go up in flames on its way towards world revolution. The structure is in the grounds of one of the big capitalist hotels. One of Siqueiros's co-workers has been Leopoldo Arenal – one of the last two people to be seen with Sheldon. Siqueiros does not want to talk now of the assassination attempt on Trotsky. He is seventy five; there are more important things to talk about; *The March of Humanity* is not finished.

Chapter 7

In May 1917 Trotsky had arrived in Petrograd – as St Petersburg was now called – when the revolution against the Tsar was ten weeks old. He had hurried from New York, where he had been lecturing and writing, via Nova Scotia, where he had been interned briefly by the British. The February revolution in Petrograd had ousted the Tsar and put into government a coalition of liberals and moderate socialists. Trotsky was certain that this would be only an interim government before the Bolsheviks took over. Lenin and other exiled Bolshevik leaders had arrived in Petrograd shortly before him.

There was an air of intense excitement in Petrograd. Crowds collected in the streets and argued. All conventions and old ideas seemed open to question: the one faith was in the revolutionary future. It seemed that at last a Marxist sun was about to rise over the hill.

Trotsky rushed to the Petrograd Soviet, of which he had been a leading member in 1905. The Soviet welcomed Trotsky, but asked which side he was on. Trotsky did not know about sides. He wanted a platform from which to speak.

The sides on the extreme left wing of Russian politics were still the Bolsheviks and Mensheviks. In the present crisis Lenin, leader of the Bolsheviks, was in favour of trying to take over power by armed insurrection; the Mensheviks, on whose side Trotsky had once been, advocated working temporarily with the present government. But now Trotsky found himself aligned with Lenin. They both had a sense of urgency – of history being on their side.

Trotsky wrote of these days in Petrograd as a "whirlpool in

which men and events swept by me as swiftly as litter on a rushing stream". One of the bits of litter was the head of the moderate government, Kerensky, who "personified the accidental in an otherwise continuous causation". Trotsky found his own activity in a stream of mass meetings. These were held everywhere – in schools, theatres, factories and streets. Trotsky's favourite platform was the Modern Circus: here "every square inch was filled, every human body compressed to its limit". He spoke "out of a warm cavern of human bodies: whenever I stretched out my hands I would touch someone . . . No speaker, no matter how exhausted, could resist the electric tension of that impassioned human throng". Sometimes he felt his words coming straight from his unconscious – "as if I were listening to the speaker from outside, trying to keep pace with his ideas, afraid that like a somnambulist he might fall off the edge of the roof at the sound of my conscious reasoning." At the end of these meetings – "The crowd was unwilling to break up . . . In a semi-conscious haze of exhaustion I had to float on countless arms above the heads of the people to reach the exit". In the crowd he would sometimes catch glimpses of the excited faces of his two daughters, whom he had scarcely seen since the time of their birth during his first exile fifteen years ago. They would reach out their hands to him, but he was carried by the mob.

Lenin spoke at meetings, but also worked steadily in the background. He had created, and was maintaining, a party machine. The power of Lenin to be the ultimate organiser and leader after the revolution lay in his ability to have something of the fire of Trotsky and yet at the same time to sit back and watch or even manipulate which way the flames blew. Trotsky had come to agree with Lenin about the need for the Bolsheviks to seize power: Lenin agreed with Trotsky's insistence on the need for "permanent" revolution – that is, the idea that revolution in Russia had to be part of a larger and continuing socialist revolution throughout Europe. Whatever difference still remained between the two lay within the nature of the facts of power. When Lenin at this time was asked what still kept him and Trotsky in some senses apart, he replied "Ambition, ambition, ambition".

During the summer of 1917 there were food shortages in Petrograd; news arrived of defeats on the front where Russia was still at war with Germany. Public feeling, needing a scapegoat, turned against the Bolsheviks. Their leaders were rumoured to be German spies: this story arose from the Germans having allowed Lenin to cross Germany from Switzerland at the time of the February revolution in a sealed train – they had thought, correctly, that his presence in Russia would weaken the Russian effort in the war. Lenin and other Bolshevik leaders decided to go into hiding. Trotsky stayed in Petrograd. He went on with his tumultuous meetings in the Modern Circus; he armed the Red Guards, or Bolshevik volunteers, to try to keep order in the streets. He was arrested by the moderate government and again went to jail: he found conditions there worse than they had been under the Tsar, though the jailers and the police seemed the same. As always, Trotsky poured out his articles and pamphlets. Another swing of the public pendulum got him out on bail – there was the threat of a right-wing militarist revival and it was felt that the Bolsheviks with their disciplined forces might be needed by the government. Trotsky hurried back to the Soviet and there, to his surprise, found the Bolsheviks in the majority. On the night of the 24th/25th October the Bolshevik revolution happened almost by itself. The government tried to close-down a revolutionary printing works: Trotsky sent a detachment of Red Guards to take it over. From there, the Red Guards took over the Telephone Exchange, the Post Offices, the Railway Stations, the Banks, the Power Stations, and the Ministries. They did this with minimum of fuss and with casualties of ten. There remained only the Winter Palace, the seat of government, which was taken the next day. Kerensky had already left the city. Trotsky remarked that the Bolsheviks' enemies "simply had failed to notice an uprising that was actually taking place".

Lenin had returned on the night of the revolution. He and

Trotsky tried to get some sleep side by side: "body and soul were relaxing like overtaut strings". Lenin always gave Trotsky credit for leading the October Revolution: Trotsky always said that without Lenin's basic work building the party and his enormous authority even when in hiding there would have been no revolution to lead. Somewhere in the background of committees and events at this time was a Bolshevik from Georgia known as Stalin, whom Trotsky described as "a grey spot which would sometimes give out a dim and inconsequential light".

The Bolsheviks found themselves in power unexpectedly. They set up government in the Smolny building. Trotsky described the scene – "decisions were made with very little discussion . . . were almost improvised . . . they were none the worse for that". He had his theory of history – "Marxism considers itself the conscious expression of the unconscious historical process. But the 'unconscious' process – in the historical-philosophical sense of the term, not in the psychological – coincides with its conscious expression only at its highest point, when the masses, by sheer elemental pressure, break through the social routine and give victorious expression to the deepest needs of historical development . . . The creative union of the conscious with the unconscious is what one usually calls 'inspiration'. Revolution is the inspired frenzy of history."

At the same time the revolution "outwardly did not look very imposing; men went about tired, hungry, and unwashed, with inflamed eyes and unshaven beards. And afterwards none of them could recall much about those critical days and hours".

The Bolsheviks proclaimed a programme of Peace, Land and Bread. Peace was to be just and democratic, Land was to be shared amongst peasants, and Bread had simply to exist and be distributed. These were fine slogans for an opposition, but more difficult for those in power. But there was the divine confidence of Marxism: when the true revolution came and the proletariat in the form of the Bolshevik party achieved power it was believed not that things ought to be correct but that in fact they were correct, in spite of any appearances to the contrary.

Amongst the masses in Russia there were two forces at this time – a small nucleus of politically-minded industrial workers who were passionately committed and ready for heroism – they had worked and waited for the revolution for years and greeted it now as the Promised Land – and an almost infinitely larger body round it of peasants and workers who remained apathetic. These latter were stirred by the revolution mainly into an orgy of drunkenness. The wine-stores in Petrograd were looted: the dedicated few struggled to prevent this. Trotsky wrote of a sailor called Markin who "fought for a sober October. Soaked to the skin, exuding the fragrance of the choicest wines ... Markin beat off the alcoholic attack of the counter-revolution".

Lenin made a show of offering Trotsky the leadership of the Bolshevik Party. Trotsky, on genuine grounds, refused. He always saw Lenin as his leader. Trotsky was made Foreign Secretary. The two men worked at opposite ends of a long corridor in the Smolny building; they improvised orders and sent messages scurrying to and fro. They lived on cabbage soup and black bread. They had to stabilise a revolution out of nothing.

Trotsky at this time was coming to the height of his powers: he "walked about like an electric battery and each contact with him brought forth a discharge". This was the description of a colleague, Lunacharsky. But Lunacharsky also wrote – "Trotsky often looks at himself. Trotsky treasures his historical role, and would undoubtedly be ready to make any personal sacrifice, not by any means excluding the sacrifice of his life, in order to remain in the memory of mankind with the halo of a genuine revolutionary leader". Of Lenin Lunacharsky wrote – "I believe that Lenin never looks at himself, never glances in the mirror of history, never even thinks of what posterity will say of him – simply does his work. He does his work imperiously, not because power is sweet to him, but because he is sure that he is right."

As Foreign Secretary, Trotsky was faced with the first of the practical and almost insoluble dilemmas of revolutionaries when they have achieved power – which can only be contained, perhaps, within a theory of dialectics. The war with Germany had resulted in almost total defeat for the Russian army; soldiers were packing up and leaving the front in thousands. The Bolsheviks had pledged themselves to end the war as a matter of both principle and expediency; yet they were also determined not to sacrifice honour, being a young party intent on world-rejuvenation. Trotsky went to Brest Litovsk to talk to the Germans: he almost did achieve the impossible simply by announcing, after months of diplomatic parleying, that the Russians would both withdraw from the war and at the same time refuse to accept degrading conditions of peace – and the Germans could do what they liked. Trotsky presented the conference with a fine dialectical slogan – Neither Peace Nor War – and left. He did not think that the Germans could logically go on attacking Russia if there was no one defending it. But the German high command had no regard for logic. They did march further into Russia, Petrograd was threatened, and in the end the Bolsheviks had to accept worse conditions than those which had been offered to them originally.

This was the first practical defeat for dialectical optimism. There had been some conflict here between Lenin and Trotsky: Lenin had wanted to accept the peace terms from the beginning and Trotsky had wanted to make the gesture: in practical terms Lenin had been right, but Trotsky's gesture had been intended to show to Socialist parties in other countries that the Bolsheviks would not play the old diplomatic game but were truly revolutionary: and in this Trotsky's attitude was effective, if only as a symbol.

This dilemma of peace and war foreshadowed, but in reverse, a dilemma which was to confront Trotsky two years later at the end of the Civil War between the Bolshevik forces and the armies of counter-revolution. Then, Trotsky and the Red Army were victorious and Trotsky, as Commissar for War, was faced with a decision about whether or not the revolution should be carried by force of arms into Europe. None of the Bolsheviks, remembering Marx, had thought that the revolution would take place only in Russia; they had believed that a workers' revolution would occur throughout industrial Europe. Marx had in fact thought Russia an unlikely area for revolution because of its industrial backwardness and thus its lack of organisation among workers. By 1920 however the revolution in Russia had not only come but was triumphant; Russia was ready to march into Poland, which had attacked it. But Marx had also said that revolution could not be spread from Europe by force of arms. The Bolshevik leaders were thus again in two minds: they had had to create an army in order to defend the revolution since the industrial workers in the rest of Europe had failed to rise in their support, but now Russia was in a position to encourage Marxism more forcibly. And this was a situation that Marx had not foreseen. The Bolsheviks marched into Poland – but were defeated. This resolved their doubts. They did not wage an aggressive war again for twenty years. Then, at the beginning and at the end of a second world war Stalin made another effort to bring Marxism up to date and marched into Europe; but by that time the orthodox Marxist faith had largely been given up anyway.

The Civil War posed another problem of violence and authority. The war was between the Red Army which Trotsky created almost out of nothing – the old Tsarist army had disappeared but after two and a half years Trotsky commanded five million men – and the White Armies of counter-revolution, which were run by almost autonomous war-lords in the Urals and in the Ukraine and in the west and consisted of semi-mercenary soldiers backed by Britain and France. Trotsky, with an immense show of personal energy, won: he travelled round the various fronts in a special armoured train: everywhere he instilled new spirit into flagging troops. By 1920 the White Armies were in retreat. Trotsky had hoped that the Red Army in its structure would be socialist and democratic; but in the emergency he had had to gather again many of the old Tsarist officers and technicians, and to make use of conscription. In order to maintain discipline in the chaos he had had to threaten not only to use the usual forms of military discipline but to take hostages from the families of deserters and potential deserters. He protested years later that the threats of the death penalty against hostages had scarcely ever been carried out. However – "I carry full responsibility for the Decree of 1919. It was a necessary measure in the struggle against the oppressors. Only in the historical context of the struggle lies the justification of the decree as in general the justification of the whole civil war which, too, can be called, not without foundation, 'disgusting barbarism'."

At the end of the Civil War Trotsky became depressed. It has sometimes been thought that he was haunted by some of the brutalities carried out in his name at the time; but there is little evidence of this in his writing. It is true that towards the end of the war he resigned as Commissar of War and had to be persuaded back to his post by a genial and inscrutable Lenin – but his withdrawal at this time could be explained by exhaustion after the energy expended during two and a half years. One of his co-travellers on his special train estimated that the sum of the length of his journeys would have taken him five times around the world. During the journeys he dictated a commentary on the events he was engaged in: this was printed as *The Defence of Terrorism*. This book is a realistic if tough analysis of the use of violence in war: "War, like revolution, is founded upon intimidation. A victorious war, generally speaking, destroys only an insignificant part of the conquered army, intimidating the remainder and breaking their will. The revolution works in the same way; it kills individuals and intimidates thousands". Once or twice Trotsky's more virulent style breaks out – "As for us, we were never concerned with the Kantian-priestly and vegetarian-Quaker prattle about the 'sacredness of human life'!

We were revolutionaries in opposition and have remained revolutionaries in power." Lenin, when reinstating Trotsky as Commissar of War, gave him a piece of paper which was an effective carte-blanche for any repressive actions he might think necessary.

There was one action that did return later to haunt Trotsky if only in the "prattle" of his enemies. This concerned a rebellion of sailors at the naval base of Kronstadt in 1921. The sailors, objecting to the continuing authoritarian Bolshevik rule, mutinied and proclaimed a new revolution. To Trotsky, as usual, was given the task of putting the revolution down; he was the man most likely to understand it as well as to defeat it. In 1917 he had been a hero to the sailors of Kronstadt; now he argued, but they would not listen. The Red Army attacked across the ice: there was a great slaughter. Years later when Trotsky was an exile in Mexico the memory of this was still brought up against him – by people who had known little of the responsibilities let alone the abuses of war.

With the beginning of peace in the early 1920's Trotsky had a new burst of optimism – "We are participants in this unprecedented historic attempt. . . . Hundreds and thousands of years of man's development and struggle will be a mockery if we do not attain a new society in which all human relations will be based on co-operation and man will be man's brother, not his enemy." But there were new and perhaps more difficult dilemmas with the peace.

The dilemma which Trotsky faced after the war was in essence the same as that which had confronted him on his first introduction to the Party in 1903 – the problem of the continuing necessity for political authority and its conflict in peacetime with freedom of expression and the right to form an opposition. In 1903 the quarrel between the Bolsheviks and the Mensheviks had resulted in a victory for the Bolshevik's policy of tight-knit control: but the problem then had been to do with a comparatively small political party out of power and not with the actual handling of power. Marx, and Marxists, had seen the coming to power of the true party of the working class as a sort of millenium – it seemed as if nothing much had to be said about this just as nothing much can be said about heaven – it was almost assumed that there would be no problem then of authority against freedom since in the "true" workers state everyone would be a worker and thus, logically, on the side of the state. But what if the workers were not logical? Marxists had never asked the question – what would happen if the Bolshevik Party came to power but did not have the backing of some, or a large part, of the workers? This question was almost unaskable, because it was against dogma.

Marx had felt passionately about freedom of expression for workers; just as he had believed in the true workers' state. But in 1921, after the privations of the Civil War, there were workers and peasants in a state of unrest – and they blamed the government. The answer to the unaskable question about who was right, the workers or the state, seemed to the Bolsheviks to be that they, the Party, knew better than the workers what the workers really wanted – much as a parent may try to make out that it knows the wants of a child better than the child itself. Trotsky, typically, was vociferous as an advocate in both conflicting attitudes at once – insisting both that freedom of expression for the workers should be guaranteed, but that in this particular case the party knew better than the workers.

It was Trotsky's burden, as well as genius, to see both sides of a question – and to proclaim these to the world. At the negotiations at Brest Litovsk he had coined the slogan – Neither Peace Nor War: now, faced with peace, it seemed as if he were saying – Both Authority And Freedom. But the country was exhausted; there was chaos and hunger; Trotsky wanted to turn the armies that he had commanded into gangs of labourers with military discipline, to make trade unions illegal (why should unions be needed in a workers state?) and to introduce compulsory service and compulsory movement of labour. To do the compelling there had, logically, to be a Party which compelled; and this, because it was doing it for the workers state, had logically to know better than the workers.

There was a paradox here in metaphysics; but in the matter of practical politics, in which a certain simple-mindedness is needed in order to pursue an aim successfully, it left Trotsky open to attack from both sides – both from those who advocated more freedom of expression and from those who advocated more centralised control. It also rendered him in himself, possibly, slightly incapacitated for the cheese-paring business of day-to-day politics. He became irritable in committees, often lost his temper, was witheringly sarcastic about those who did not have his own ability or taste for dialectics. He made many enemies. There thus began now, when he had tasted both the passion of revolutionary opposition and the strength of power, a pattern that was to dominate the second half of his political life – that of being in theory often right but in practice, except in times of revolution and war, having to see ranged against him those whose thinking was superficial and whose motives were often cowardly but whose policies, even in Marxist terms, seemed to work. It was as if he were being driven to face in his experience the fact that political principles, if pursued truly, result in paradoxes that perhaps can be held in a lively and complex way only in the mind: that it is by the betrayal of them by the deadly and monolithic state that the implementation of at least some of them becomes possible.

Chapter 8

During the summer of 1940 the walls at Coyoacan were heightened and new watchtowers and alarm-bells were installed and steel doors and windows were put around Trotsky's bedroom like bulkheads. Trotsky would walk about the garden and make suggestions. He would say – "It reminds me of my first prison at Khirghizan. The doors make the same sound when they shut. It's not a home, it's a medieval prison."

After the May 24th raid the number of guards was increased and discipline was tightened. Trotsky worked at his writing and dictation: he meticulously looked after his cacti, his chickens and and his rabbits. His work at this time was mostly to do with the May 24th raid – gathering information, analysing it, pouring out refutations and suggestions to press and the police. Often in the mornings he would make a joke about still being alive: he would say to Natalya "Another day, Natasha, by courtesy of Stalin!" Natalya ran the austere house and did the housekeeping; Seva, aged thirteen, went to and fro from school. Sometimes in the evening the guards and Seva would play games; this annoyed Trotsky, who did not like to see time wasted.

Trotsky liked doing the dirty jobs around the house: if the plumbing went wrong, he would mend it. He would not ask anyone else to do what he would not do himself. Sometimes pigeons flew into the trip wires and set off the alarm bells. Trotsky did not sleep well: he continued to take sleeping powders.

He did not often go out of the house and garden at this time; only to his dentist, or very seldom now on a trip to the mountains. When travelling through the streets he would hold a handkerchief over the lower part of his face and try to be incognito; but people would recognise him and call out "Trotsky! Trotsky!" On the journeys to the mountains he had once loved the drives over rough roads; he said they reminded him of the Civil War in Russia. Now, on a journey after the May 24th raid, he slept much of the time in the car. Once or twice he kept to his room for two or three days and lay in the dark; only Natalya went in to him. His fevers recurred, which had begun at the time of the death of Lenin.

Fewer people came to visit him in 1940. With the war, travel was difficult between Europe and Mexico. His secretaries and devotees came and went from America; each new guard, such as Sheldon Harte, was a new mind for him to take hold of and try to mould. But young Americans were seldom hard enough stones for him to sharpen his own mind on. Occasionally old friends such as the Rosmers managed to come from Europe; they had brought Seva with them in 1939. He could talk with them about politics in Europe. But even to sophisticated Communists he had become somewhat unnerving. André Breton, the French poet, had visited him in 1938 and afterwards had written that in Trotsky's presence had had felt himself so inadequate that he was afraid he had a "Cordelia complex". Trotsky had replied "Your eulogies seem so exaggerated that I am becoming a little uneasy about the future of our relations." For companionship for the most past he relied upon Natalya. For the rest, there was work.

He read an enormous number of newspapers – *The Times*, the *New York Times*, *Le Temps*, as well as Russian and Mexican papers. He would underline anything that interested him in blue or red pencil. He carried on a huge correspondence in Russian, French, German, Spanish and English – in all of which languages he was reasonably fluent. He had an old fashioned dictating machine which scratched words on to wax cylinders. He was annoyed at having to spend so much time on the May 24th raid; he wanted to get back to his biography of Stalin. But even this work, unfinished at the time of his death, seemed to become infected by some of the slanging-match style in which he himself was being bombarded by the Mexican press.

The articles he wrote were published on pamphlets or in the Trotskyite magazine *The Fourth International*. This magazine had been founded in 1938 in New York. When Trotsky had first come to Mexico there had been dissident voices amongst his American followers on questions of central importance to Marxism. Trotsky had set out to answer these.

Marx, Trotsky said, had seen "the development of human society" as "the history of the succession of various systems of economy". "The primitive commune was either superseded or supplemented by slavery; slavery was succeeded by serfdom with its feudal superstructure; the commercial development of cities brought Europe in the sixteenth century to the capitalist order." "The transition from one system to another was always determined by the growth of the productive forces; i.e., of technique and organisation of labour."

Under capitalism, Trotsky explained, Marx had said that "commodities are exchanged for each other in a given ratio, at first directly and eventually through the medium of gold or money. The basic property of commodities . . . is the human labour expended on them". The capitalist buys labour power, which "like all other commodities, is evaluated according to the quantity of labour invested in it, i.e., of those means of subsistence which are necessary for the survival and the reproduction of the worker". But the consumption of that commodity – labour power – results in "values" which are "greater than those which the worker himself receives and which he expends for his upkeep. The capitalist buys labour power in order to exploit it".

"That part of the product which goes to cover the workers own subsistence Marx calls the necessary-product; that part which the worker produces above this is the surplus-product." Thus – "the class struggle is nothing else than the struggle for surplus-product. He who owns surplus product is the master of the situation."

Marx thought that as a result of this competitive struggle capital would become concentrated in fewer and fewer hands, and that along with this there would grow "the mass of misery, oppression, slavery, degredation, exploitation, to ever greater lengths". "But with this too there grows the revolt of the working class, a class always increasing in numbers, and disciplined, united and organised by the very mechanism of the process of capitalist production itself." This working class would finally take over power simply because it would recognise the situation and there would be nothing else for it to do. "To Marx, the problem of reconstituting society did not arise from some prescription motivated by his personal predelictions; it followed as an iron-clad historical necessity."

This was Trotsky's exposition of Marx. But there were criticisms that could be made of it – reflecting both on Trotsky and on Marx. Marx originally had been moved by "personal predelictions": his political passions had been aroused by the terrible predicament of the poor in Europe in the 1840's; and it was the dogmatic structuring of the time that drove him "necessarily" to force his passions into a "scientific" theory. But more important than this, the "historical necessity" of which he spoke did not in fact seem to be occurring.

This was what worried Trotskyites in New York at the end of the 1930's. Two of the leaders, James Burnham and Max Shachtman, broke away from Trotsky. Burnham wrote about Marxism "I regard these beliefs as either false or obsolete or meaningless"; he foresaw capitalist society being taken over not by the workers but by an ever increasing bureaucracy – a new class that would exploit others in the state. This in fact seemed to be happening both in Europe and America. Trotsky, in his replies, found himself involved in his usual vituperation; he sneered at the New Yorkers as "intellectual snobs"; he asked how they, the intelligentsia, could be expected to know about workers. But he did not trouble to answer Burnham or Shachtman very deeply. It was then that he had written of his own doubts concerning Marxism: it might conceivably be, he said, that the hopes which Marxism placed in the proletariat had been false: in that case "We could be compelled to acknowledge that (Stalinist bureaucracy) was rooted not in the backwardness of the country . . . but in the congenital incapacity of the proletariat to become a ruling class. . . . Nothing else would remain but to recognise openly that the socialist programme, based on the internal contradictions of capitalist society, had petered out as Utopia".

Having pointed out this possibility, Trotsky immediately and typically countered it by saying that he did not think it would happen; the proletariat would be stirred to its historic senses by the Second World War. But in this he was pinning his faith on cataclysm; on the circumstances in which he himself had flourished twenty years ago, and then had found himself stranded.

The other criticism of him from his followers at this time were to do with his role in the old war: his critics dug up the stories about the taking of hostages and the putting-down of the rebellion at Krondstadt; they asked with, as Trotsky put it, "double their usual amount of moral effluvia" – what difference was there, morally, between the ruthlessness of Stalinism and that of Trotskyism? Trotsky answered them in a pamphlet called *Their Morals And Ours*. He explained – to say that the moral basis of his actions was no different from that of Stalin's was to ignore "the material foundation of the various currents – their class nature and by that token their objective historical role". Thus – "shooting a mad dog which threatens a child" is a virtue: "shooting with the aim of violation or murder" is a crime. The end, that is, justifies the means: and the end is justified if, as it does in Trotskyism, it "unites the revolutionary proletariat . . . imbues them with a sense of their own historic mission, raises their courage and spirit of self-sacrifice in the struggle . . . leads to increasing the power of man over nature and to the abolition of the power of man over man". Stalinism on the other hand "re-establishes the most offensive form of privileges, imbues inequality with a provocative character, strangles mass self-activity under police absolutism, transforms administration into a monopoly of the Kremlin oligarchy and regenerates the fetichism of power in forms that absolute monarchy dared not dream of." And finally – "A slave-owner who through cunning or violence shackles a slave in chains and a slave who through cunning or violence breaks the chains – let not the contemptible eunuchs tell us that they are equals before the court of morality!"

Trotsky won the argument; but still did not answer the questions deeply. He admitted – "The theory of eternal morals can in no way survive without God". And when he was challenged about his role in the Krondstadt rebellion nearly twenty years ago he replied wearily – "I do not know . . . whether there were any innocent victims . . . I cannot undertake to decide now, so long after the event, who should have been punished and in what way . . . I am ready to admit that civil war is not a school of human behaviour. Idealists and pacifists have always blamed revolution for 'excesses'. The crux of the matter is that the 'excesses' spring from the very nature of revolution, which is itself an 'excess' of history. Let those who wish to reject in their petty journalistic articles revolution on this ground. I do not reject it".

In the argument about ends justifying means he had quoted the instance of a Bolshevik leader called Kirov who had been assassinated in 1934. There had been a mystery about this: Stalin had claimed that the assassin was a Trotskyite; there was evidence afterwards that the murder had been engineered by Stalin himself. The assassination was the pretext for the start of the whole series of Stalin's trials and purges in the late thirties. From Mexico, in *Our Morals and Theirs*, Trotsky wrote – "The assassinated Kirov, a rude satrap, does not call forth any sympathy. Our relation to the assassin remains neutral only because we do not know what motives guided him. If it became known that Nicolayev (the assassin) acted as a conscious avenger

77

for the workers' rights trampled on by Kirov, our sympathies would be fully on the side of the assassin."

One of the occasional visitors to the house in Coyoacan during the early months of 1940 was a girl who had been a friend of the Rosmers in Paris and who was known as an ardent Trotskyite. She was an American from Brooklyn, called Sylvia Agelof. She had arrived in Mexico in January and had brought messages to Coyoacan. She stayed in the city and occasionally came to help with the secretarial work. She had worked as an interpreter at the founding conference of Trotsky's Fourth International in Paris in 1938.

She had a boyfriend with her in Mexico City who was known to her as Jacques Mornard – supposedly the son of a Belgian diplomat, born in Teheran in 1904. She had met him in Paris at the time of the Fourth International; he had been working there, he had said, as a free-lance journalist. He had taken her out in Paris and she had become his mistress. When she returned to America early in 1939 he had promised to follow her. He did so in September, travelling with a false Canadian passport under the name of Frank Jacson. He was doing this, he said, because he was avoiding the Belgian call-up.

The two of them were living in a hotel in the middle of the city in the spring of 1940. Sometimes Mornard would drive Sylvia out to Coyoacan and fetch her when she had done her secretarial tasks. He did not at first seem to want to go in through the gates: he let it be known he was not interested in politics. He worked for an import/export firm, he said, and was thus a capitalist. However he became friendly with the guards, with whom he would chat over the walls. And he would sometimes greet Seva on his way home from school. To the Trotskys he was known by hearsay as Frank Jacson – Sylvia's husband.

No one thought much of making enquiries about Mornard. There was little reason why they should. As Trotsky himself used to say – if the credentials of every visitor to the house were checked for political reliability he would not have much chance of seeing many visitors; during the twenties and thirties political fashions had changed frequently and most left-wing sympathisers had skeletons in their cupboards which they would not want looked at too closely. And Mornard was that relatively harmless thing in Communist politics at the time – a capitalist. After the May 24th raid it was against Communists' own internecine passions that Trotsky was being guarded. And as he had also said at the time of the enquiries into Sheldon Harte – if an agent of the G.P.U. really wanted to get in, no precautions could ultimately prevent him even "worming his way into the guard".

In any case, Sylvia Agelof was a loyal admirer of Trotsky's and her boy-friend Jacques was just someone who sometimes hung around outside the gates. It was peculiar, perhaps, that Sylvia was quiet and not very attractive and Jacques was dashing and debonair. But such considerations as this were beyond the scope of materialistic politics. Jacques let hints drop to the guards that he might be able to help Trotsky; although it was war-time he still had one or two contacts with Europe. And he explained how he admired Trotsky as a man – it was only in politics that he was not interested. He disarmed suspicion by a mixture of reticence and yet tentatively appearing to be useful.

It is unlikely that the G.P.U. planned such tactics exactly. Secret organisations are often credited with miracles of planning and foresight – perhaps just because they remain secret. Jacques Mornard, hesitant outside the walls, was probably caught between two impulses of mind as Sheldon Harte had been and as were many young men at the time. Bewilderment, and the sudden determination to be rid of doubts and unbearably conflicting tendencies at any cost, are as good ways as some of describing dialectically the inexorable march of history.

Chapter 9

Trotsky is sometimes credited with the founding of the G.P.U., but there is no evidence for this except that at the time of the Revolution and just after he and Lenin were responsible in Russia for almost everything. When the Bolsheviks found it necessary to set up a political police – there were of course non-workers reluctant to welcome the workers' state – they called it the CHEKA, or more mellifluously The Extraordinary Commission For The Struggle Against Counter-Revolution. But the counter revolutionaries they were struggling against were then outside the party – White Guards, Mensheviks, Anarchists, and so on – and the Bolsheviks did not have to worry too much about dilemmas. The Bolshevik in charge of these operations was Dzerzhinsky – a man of "deep poetic sensibility, constantly stirred to compassion for the weak and suffering". These are words of Isaac Deutscher, Trotsky's admirable biographer. At the same time, Deutscher says, "his devotion to his cause was so intense that it made him a fanatic who would shrink from no act of terror so long as he was convinced it was necessary for the cause. Living in permanent tension between his lofty idealism and the butchery which was his daily job, high strung, his life-force burning itself out like a flame, he was regarded by his comrades as the strange 'saint of the revolution'."

During the Civil War the G.P.U. was a specialist branch of the armed forces. But then when the war was over most of its responsible officers left and it became a resort for – in Dzerzhinsky's own word – scoundrels. And its victims became more and more those inside the party; those outside had been defeated. The name CHEKA changed to G.P.U. – State Political Board.

The story of the increasing power of the G.P.U. during the twenties runs parallel to the decline in Trotsky's political fortunes – and indeed to those of orthodox Marxism. From the time of Lenin's first illness in 1922 (he had a stroke and for a time lost the power of speech) the man politically in the ascendant was Stalin – of whom, Trotsky said, hardly anyone had heard before the revolution; he was "the outstanding mediocrity of the party". Stalin had been secretary to the party's Central Committee; he had had control over appointments to jobs and to committees; he had manipulated the powers of patronage and propaganda quietly, from the background, until he had control of the party machine. And this meant working through the G.P.U. In a totalitarian state which has done away with the framework of political traditions the final arbiters of power always become the political figurehead – either manipulating or manipulated – and the secret police. Each has its aura of terror about it; the former as a sort of devil or god just because as a character he has to be enigmatic – has to be some sort of vacuum, however crafty, which other people's fantasies can rush in to fill – and the latter because they can literally like a magician make their opponents disappear with a flick of the finger in the middle of the night. Totalitarian terror is both actual and psychological. Trotsky found himself in opposition to these tendencies in policy and by instinct. He had known something of the totalitarianism of power – and of its dangers.

So long as Lenin was still alive the problem did not come to a head; Lenin was too much of a leader even when ill for Stalin to do anything but prepare in the background. But Lenin had been a leader in revolution and war: there was now the question of what happened to revolution in peace. If there was not the sort of authority that Stalin and the G.P.U. seemed to be moving towards what sort of authority was there? Old traditions of government were over; and the proletariat, upon whom Marxist faith had been pinned, did not seem to be living up to the expectation of their becoming angels. In the meantime there had to be some rule. It had come to be accepted that the Bolshevik party was to rule – that the party stood for the workers in a way in which the workers could not stand for themselves – and that in order to preserve itself and the revolution the party had had to do away with opposition, since the situation was too tense to allow this.

But the creation of a single-party system meant that not only did the voices of enemies seem to be silenced but those of friends. With the beginning of an atmosphere of terror there was nothing much of interest that could be said by anyone; no discussion, however constructively intended, could be risked; there was no platform outside the system from which to criticise it and any critical thought or effort could be called treacherous. And thus the system itself, like a body without exercise, seemed to grow stale. There were enough sluggish minds within the party to welcome this.

With this sluggishness came a misuse of thought and language; the aim of a statement began to be concerned not with truth nor relevance to facts but with the power to self-justify or compel. The will of the Bolshevik party was what mattered because this will was the will of the proletariat – criticism of the Bolshevik party became treachery to the proletariat. After a time, in this usage, language became a noise which even the person using it ceased to care what it meant – there was nothing to measure it by, no framework outside the will. It was a sign just of fitting-in; or of compulsion.

Lenin, from his sickbed, brooded on this. He dictated his last testament. He saw that after his death the revolution would proceed in the direction personified either by Stalin or by Trotsky. Possibly, it might not proceed at all.

"I think that . . . the basic factors in the problem of stability are such members of the Central Committee as Stalin and Trotsky. In my view the relationship between them constitutes a good half of the danger of a split. . . . Having become General Secretary, Comrade Stalin has acquired immense power in his hands, and I am not certain he will always know how to use this power with sufficient caution. On the other hand Comrade Trotsky . . . is distinguished not only by his remarkable abilities: personally he is, no doubt the most able person in the present Central Committee; but he also has excessive self-confidence, and is overly attracted by the purely administrative aspect of affairs."

In a P.S. Lenin added "Stalin is too rude, and this fault, quite tolerable in our midst or in relations amongst communists, becomes intolerable for one who holds the office of General Secretary. Therefore I propose to the comrades that they consider a means of removing Stalin from the post and appointing to it another person who in all other respects differs from Stalin in one advantage alone, namely, that he is more patient, more loyal, more polite and more considerate to comrades . . ."

Why Lenin had said that Trotsky was "overly attracted by the purely administrative aspect of affairs" is a mystery; except perhaps in that during these years Trotsky had buried himself in routine work in order to hide from himself the problems of peace. Also he was increasingly involving himself in studies outside politics – in literature, in science and in philosophy. During these years he became Russia's leading literary critic. The range of his interest was immense – he wrote articles on Freud, Futurist poetry, Constructivist architecture and Shakespearian tragedy; he studied chemistry and physics and foretold the releasing of energy from the atom; he wrote homilies on mundane affairs – on family life, manners, morals. His theme was both the diversity and the unity of knowledge – man's task was to be "co-ordinator and master of all manifestations of energy". He had a vision again of a Marxist heaven in which "Man will grow incomparably stronger, wiser, subtler, his body will become more harmonious; his movements more rhythmical; his voice more musical. The forms of his existence will acquire a dynamic theatrical quality. The average man will rise to the stature of Aristotle, Goethe, Marx. And above these heights new peaks will rise".

In the meantime he did not seem to mind that he was being driven more into the background in politics. The Bolshevik Old Guard were at this time being built up as demi-gods by official historians: Trotsky stood apart from this: he saw, as usual, too many sides to too many questions. And he was not quite trusted by the party; he had always been a bit of a trouble-maker; superior, and too clever by half. And again the question was asked – Whose side was he on? As Lenin's illness grew worse the people around began jockeying for position. There was Zinoviev, who, in Trotsky's words "climbed easily to the seventh heaven but when things took a bad turn he usually stretched himself out on a sofa; he had no intermediate moods, it was either seventh heaven or the sofa". There was Kamenev, from whom one could not expect "either independence of judgment or initiative in action": and Bukharin, whom "you must always keep your eyes on, or else he will succumb quite imperceptibly to the influence of someone directly opposite you as other people fall under an automobile". There was also, of course, Stalin, waiting for just such eventualities. Trotsky's hostility to Stalin was in the open by now: "I was repelled by those very qualities that were his strength on the wave of a decline – the narrowness of his interest, his empiricism, the coarseness of his psychological make-up; his peculiar cynicism of a provincial whom Marxism has freed from any prejudices without, however, replacing them with a philosophical outlook thoroughly thought-out and mentally assimilated".

Zinoviev, Kamenev and Stalin formed a secret block round the dying Lenin to keep Trotsky out of power. Trotsky was the obvious successor to Lenin: he had been his right-hand-man for years. Lenin had shown his preference for Trotsky in his will – he had even once offered to make Trotsky officially his deputy but Trotsky had declined this. The triumvirate of Stalin, Zinoviev and Kamenev were obviously jealous of Trotsky; they were separated from him not so much by policy as by temperament; Trotsky was advocating policies which later they themselves were

84

to adopt. But there was nevertheless some reason in their plotting. The revolution had been held together by the personality of one man: when Lenin died, there would inevitably be a period of disruption. During this period there would be required some steadfast unifying control and Trotsky had never been politically unifying, and was to his own unique vision steadfast. He did not seem himself to be interested, also, in taking over from Lenin.

During a Sunday in 1923 Trotsky went out duck shooting on the river Dubna. Walking back he stepped into a bog and got cold feet. He had to keep to his bed with influenza, and later with what was described as a "cryptogenic temperature".

Trotsky lay in the Kremlin. Lenin lay paralysed in the country. Their colleagues got on with politics.

Years later when Trotsky asked the question "How could you have lost power?" he wrote of the political atmosphere of the early 1920's.

"A division began to reveal itself between the leaders who expressed the historical line of the class and could see beyond the apparatus, and the apparatus itself – a huge, cumbrous, hetero-geneous thing that easily sucked in the average communist." Within this apparatus people began to show "an attitude of moral relaxation, or self-content and triviality. People began to feel an urge to pour out these new moods upon each other – moods in which the element of philistine gossip came to have a very prominent place. . . . If I took no part in the amusements that were becoming more and more common in the lives of the new governing stratum, it was not for moral reasons, but because I hated to inflict such boredom on myself. The visiting at each others homes, the assiduous attendance at the ballet, the drinking parties at which people who were absent were pulled to pieces, had no attraction for me. The new ruling group felt that I did not fit in with this way of living, and they did not even try to win me over. It was for this very reason that many group conversations would stop the moment I appeared, and those engaged in them would cut them short with a certain shamefacedness and a slight bitterness towards me. This was, if you like, a definite indication that I had begun to lose power."

Trotsky did make an effort to change the atmosphere by appealing over the heads of the party bureaucrats to the workers. In December 1923 he addressed an Open Letter to Party Meetings – but this was more in the style of a rallying-call to those who would join him in opposition than of a programme for an alternative government.

"Away with passive obedience, with mechanical levelling by the authorities, with suppression of personality, with servility and with careerism! A Bolshevik is not merely a disciplined man; he is a man who in each case and on each question forges a firm opinion of his own, and defends it courageously and independently not only against his enemies but inside his own party. Today perhaps he will be in a minority . . . he will submit . . . but this does not always signify that he is in the wrong. Perhaps he has seen or has understood a new task or the necessity for a turn earlier than others have done. He will persistently raise the question a second, a third, a tenth time, if need be. Thereby, he will render his party a service helping it to meet the new task fully armed, or to carry out the necessary turn without organic upheaval and without factional convulsions."

In January 1924 his doctors ordered Trotsky to go for a cure to the Black Sea: his high and mysterious temperature had stayed with him most of the autumn. He was in a train making the slow journey to the south when the news reached him of Lenin's death. The message came in the form of a telegram from Stalin. Trotsky telegraphed back enquiring whether he should return for the funeral. Stalin replied that the funeral was on the next day, so there would not be time. Trotsky continued his journey to the sea. In fact the funeral was two days later, and Trotsky's absence was taken by most people to be deliberate.

Trotsky spent "long days on the balcony facing the sea . . . over the palms and the sea reigned silence, sparkling under the blue canopy". He looked back on the days when he had fought for the revolution with Lenin. He did not have much heart, at the moment, for the future. In Moscow the triumvirate of Stalin, Zinoviev and Kamenev stepped up a campaign of calumny against him. His Open Letter had been greeted with some enthusiasm by party workers: the triumvirate replied by accusing him of being a reactionary, a traitor, a petty bourgeois – a Menshevik! Trotsky ruminated on what seemed to be the impossibility of power – on how to combine, politically, control with dignity and freedom.

His vision of the emergence into power of cocktail-party philistines was mirrored by a glimpse underneath of other forces appearing which seemed to be, like rats, inevitable complements to the over-ripeness above. The revolution had staked its faith in a world that was to come – the world of the harmonious workers' state. Now, when this other world should be becoming flesh but wasn't, there seemed to be growing from the ground on which dragon's teeth had been sowed a race not of angels but of faceless seedy furies. These, the counterpart of the grandiose philistines above, were the violent enemies – the progeny of revolution that could not be admitted. With the failure of the imagined god-like worker there seemed to have emerged into the vacuum an antithesis of this god – the member of the proletariat who, having been told that he had power and not experiencing it, yet had to exercise the mechanisms of power because that was what he was there for. Propping up the leadership, that is, there was the G.P.U. Its members cared nothing for what Trotsky had called the "suppression of personality" because they had no personality to suppress; they were components of a machine at the same time mindless and violent. But still occasionally charming. They were the inevitable servants of the cult of the philistines – everything idealistic being gnawed by its opposite. Trotsky saw this, felt it; knew perhaps that it might be unstoppable but that it was against this that for the rest of his life he would have to fight. But he was too much of a politician ever wholly and consciously to admit that the battle was mainly this

– admit, that is, that there is something in ordinary men, of whatever class, even that which has been liberated by revolution, which sometimes flourishes upon destruction; and that this perhaps can only be dealt with, if at all, by some knowledge and custom beyond those of materialist interest.

But this could possibly explain why, nearly twenty years later, when a stranger called Jacques Mornard turned up outside his gates in Mexico Trotsky could at the same time both be totally prepared for an assassin and yet not be able to expose him when he met him face to face.

Chapter 10

Ramon Mercader was a Spaniard born in Barcelona in 1914, ten years after the fictitious Belgian Jacques Mornard – and it is striking that a man who could pretend for a large part of his life to be someone other than who he was could also make out that he was ten years older than he was; and that no one, ever, seemed to notice or to care.

Ramon was the son of a powerful mother, Caridad, and a conventional father, Pablo. They had split up when Ramon was eleven. His mother, a native of Cuba, had had artistic pretensions; she had once tried to be a novice nun. His father had accepted bourgeois standards unquestioningly.

Ramon went to school in Barcelona at the English Institute and then with the Episcopalian Fathers. His childhood coincided with a period of anarchist bomb-throwing in Catalonia. In 1925 Caridad left Barcelona and took the children to Toulouse. Pablo followed her. Caridad once or twice tried to commit suicide.

Ramon, as a young boy, ran back to Barcelona and got a job as assistant chef at the Barcelona Ritz. Caridad moved to Paris and became the mistress there of leading Communists.

In 1935 Ramon became involved in revolutionary politics in Barcelona; he joined a cell called The Cervantes Artistic Circle; he was arrested and spent three months in jail. In 1936 he was amnestied by a Popular Front government. When the Spanish Civil War started he was joined by his mother Caridad, and they both became members of the Republican Army fighting Franco.

Caridad was wounded at the front while leading an attack; she was sent on a fund-raising expedition to Mexico. Ramon became a political commissar; he worked side by side with army officers, keeping an eye on them. In 1937 Caridad returned to Spain and became the mistress of the high-ranking official in the G.P.U. called Leonid Eitigon or Eitingon or Eitington. This was the apparition also known as Sakhov, Valery, Comrade Pablo or General Kotov. Ramon Mercader was sent by General Kotov to a school for saboteurs in Spain which had recently been opened by a General Orlov – who was apparently different from General Kotov.

Any story of spies and secret agents is suspect, because it is the job of such people to tell lies and one of the few ways in which they seem completely professionally competent is this one of making their grim work appear farcical. A secret agent lives in a fevered world in which the only relief is that provided by his grandiose illusions; it is by means of these that his reality remains secret.

The story of Ramon Mercader and of his entourage has been pieced together by other investigators and comes mainly from the personal statements of spies who were later arrested and who have talked: thus there is a lot of hearsay, but every now and then hard facts. Ramon Mercader officially disappears from history in 1937: he is said to have graduated from his school for spies in Spain to a senior establishment in Moscow: he then reappears (but this is still unofficial) in 1938 transmogrified into Jacques Mornard in Paris where he had come to be introduced to Sylvia Agelof. The actual man – Ramon Mercader or Jacques Mornard – is the man who is said to be alive today (1972) in Prague or Moscow; he still denies he is Ramon Mercader and claims to be Jacques Mornard; but he knows nothing about Belgium and has been proved not to have been born in Teheran. His finger-prints are those of Mercader – but it is possible of course that the man in Prague is not the same as the man whose fingerprints were shown to be those of Mercader, or that Mercader's fingerprints were substituted for those of an actual Jacques Mornard. In the secret service world nothing finally can be certain – except of course, killing. With a corpse, there are no more transmutations possible: a job has, beyond question, been done.

In Moscow Mercader was trained to kill Trotsky.

The battle which Trotsky fought against Stalin's political leadership in the nineteen twenties was against Stalin but also against the emergence of just such a man as Mercader. It was perhaps because of figures like this appearing instead of the dedicated party worker of dreams that Trotsky had seemed so reluctant to fight for power: some such man inevitably goes with dictatorial power and Trotsky was subtle enough to feel this. So he became the leader of opposition and protest – his immense energy returned as soon as there did not seem much chance of his getting power – and he flung himself into the battle against Stalin and his henchmen – against the Eitigons, the General Orlovs, the Ramon Mercaders. He fought them in Moscow, across the length of Russia, over a large part of Europe, until in Mexico they finally caught up with him and killed him.

Politically the battle with Stalin in the middle and late twenties was to do, first, with the question of whether there could be socialism in just one country – which Marx had said there could not be but which there evidently now was (and consolidation of this socialism was the policy that Stalin advocated) – or whether there should be pursued Trotsky's idea of "permanent revolution", which was an elaboration of the original Marxist belief that socialism to be workable would necessarily have to spread throughout the world. The elaboration extended into Trotsky's second area of battle with Stalin which was about whether a privileged bureaucracy had to be introduced into the workers' state simply to keep things going – the country, after the civil war, was breaking up – or whether the old faith should be clung to of a state in which government and party officials were just democratically elected by, and on an equal footing with, the workers. By this means the atmosphere of revolution would be maintained. In both these cases Stalin, who had taken on the business of actually running the country, advocated the courses which might enable him to do this; and Trotsky, in opposition, advocated the course which was correct according to Marxist theory and optimistic but which no one yet had been able to make work. The international proletariat were not in fact carrying out permanent revolution by rising in sympathy with their Russian counterparts, and without a bureacracy inside Russia there was chaos.

Trotsky during the years of argument sometimes sat silent – in the Party Central Committee he was once seen to be reading a French novel – and sometimes fought with ferocity. Zinoviev and Kamenev saw Stalin gathering more and more power into his own hands; they realised that this would lead before long to a personal dictatorship. They changed sides, coming to Trotsky – but too late. Trotsky's fevers seemed to return to him at moments when his fight might have been effective; he was ill during the winters of 1924 and 1925 and went on a cure to Berlin in 1926; he himself wrote – "my high temperature paralyses me at the most critical moments and acted as my opponents' most steadfast ally". But he was sickened by betrayals and intrigues. And felt the workers slipping away from him. After so many wars, they seemed scared of the bogey of his "permanent revolution"; they seemed to prefer to hope for stability from Stalin's bureaucrats. Trotsky began to look again to the proletariat of industrial Europe from where Marx had said would come the true revolution. Sometimes he turned on his calumniators – he was still a powerfully mythical figure even if politically he had been edged out – and answered them in the same tones as those in which they spoke. Language became more violent as the arguments became politically more abstruse. Dzerzhinsky, the head of the G.P.U., after one screaming speech in the Party Congress fell down dead. Trotsky and his supporters in congresses and committees were increasingly heckled and shouted down; outside they found their meetings broken up by thugs. One of the oddities of this time was the way in which political language relied on terms from the French Revolution: there were innumerable reference to "Thermidorians" and "Jacobins" – those who advocated bureaucracy as opposed to those who clung to the vision of the workers' state – as if by the pompous use of these words of which hardly anyone knew the historical meaning there could be hidden the intended sense, which was usually personal abuse. Trotsky himself, in 1927, at a meeting of the Politbureau, made himself heard above the barrage of slogans and vituperation and yelled at Stalin "You are the gravedigger of the revolution!" Stalin jumped to his feet and rushed out of the meeting slamming the door.

Trotsky made one more effort to appeal to the workers in Leningrad and Moscow above the heads of the Party leaders: he was cheered in the streets, but his meetings were disrupted by gangs. A policeman fired a shot at his car; a drunken fireman jumped on the running board and put his axe through the window.

One of Trotsky's friends and colleagues, Joffe, committed suicide in 1927. He left a letter to Trotsky in which he said:

"Politically, you were always right, beginning with 1905, and I told you repeatedly that with my own ears I had heard Lenin admit that even in 1905 you, and not he, were right . . . But you have abandoned your rightness for the sake of an over-valued agreement, or compromise. This is a mistake. I repeat: politically you have always been right and now more right than ever. Some day the party will realise it, and history will not fail to accord recognition. Then don't lose your courage if someone leaves you now, or if not as many come to you, and not as soon, as you would like. You are right, but the guarantee of the victory of your rightness lies in nothing but the extreme unwillingness to yield, the strictest straightforwardness, the absolute rejection of all compromise: in this very thing lay the secret of Lenin's victories. Many a time I have wanted to tell you this, but only now have I brought myself to do so, as a last farewell!"

Trotsky's compromise had been perhaps simply to go on sitting in the Central Committee – even with a French novel.

But now the time had come for him to go. Stalin felt secure enough in his solitary seat of power; he was about to launch on a drive to consolidate his socialism-in-one-country by means of his increasing bureaucracy; he was to implement his plans for the industrialisation of the economy and for the collectivisation of agriculture which were to carry him through to the nineteen thirties leaving a mountain of corpses in their train. And for this he did not want any opposition. Industrialisation and collectivisation had been plans which Trostky had advocated: it was true that the country seemed on the edge of counter-revolution and something had to be done – transport had broken down, the peasants were not selling their food, there was hunger in the towns and party agents were murdered when they went to the country to interfere. But to the end of his life Trotsky believed that action could have been taken without the cost that Stalin and his henchmen accepted – or he said he believed this. He said that the situation could have been taken in hand by elected committees of workers. But he was out of power, and this was easy to say. And the men who had power were waiting to be rid of him.

At the Party Congress at the end of 1927 Stalin had a resolution passed that Trotsky, in view of his opposition to the Party, should be exiled to Turkestan – a Russian province near the border with China. On 16th January, 1928 he was packed and waiting in his apartment in Moscow for the G.P.U. to fetch him when a message came through that his journey had been put off for two days – there had been a demonstration in his favour at the station. Students had hung on to the engine of the train and had stopped it moving. Trotsky and Natalya were having breakfast the next day when the doorbell rang and G.P.U. poured in. Trotsky protested – what about the two days? A G.P.U. agent "good-humouredly" stopped him using the telephone. Natalya described the scene – "L.D. refused to leave of his own accord. He took advantage of the occasion to make the situation perfectly clear. The Politbureau was trying to make his exile seem

94

like a voluntary affair. It was in this light that the exile was being represented to the workers. Now it was necessary to explode this legend, and to show the reality in such a way that the facts could be neither suppressed nor distorted. Hence L.D.'s decision to compel his opponents to an open use of force. We locked ourselves in our rooms. . . . Parleys with the G.P.U. were carried on through locked doors. The agents did not know what to do; they hesitated, consulted their chiefs by telephone, and when they had received instructions announced that they were going to force the door since they must carry out their orders. Meantime L.D. was dictating instructions for the future conduct of the opposition. The door remained locked. We heard a hammer-blow, the glass crashed, and a uniformed arm was thrust inside. 'Shoot me, Comrade Trotsky, shoot me!' Kishkin, a former officer who had often accompanied L.D. on his trips to the front, kept saying excitedly.

" 'Don't talk nonsense, Kishkin!' L.D. replied calmly. 'No one is going to shoot you!' "

This was the start of Trotsky's banishment. The G.P.U. agents carried him in their arms to the train. He was followed by Natalya and their two sons, Lyova and Sergei, who struggled with the police. At the station Lyova ran towards some railway workers and cried "Comrades, see how they are carrying Comrade Trotsky away!" But the workers were apathetic. They had seen this sort of thing before; and besides, there were too many police.

95

Chapter 11

At Alma Ata in Turkestan Trotsky for a while flourished; he was able to do some of the things he had always wanted to do but for which he had not had time; he rode, fished, went on hunting expeditions in icy weather staying out for several days. He wrote "I enjoyed enormously this temporary lapse into barbarism, this sleeping in the open air, eating mutton cooked in a pail under the sky, not washing or undressing and consequently not dressing . . ." His quarry was duck. He wrote to a friend – "I decided to make a non-agression pact with the tigers".

He and Natalya and Lyova spent the summer in a thatched farmhouse in an orchard. Natalya wrote – "We watched the fruit ripen and took an active part in gathering it . . . the orchard was fragrant with apples and pears; bees and wasps were buzzing. We were making preserves."

At the same time – "L.D. was dictating a criticism of the programme of the Communist International, making corrections and handing it back for retyping. The mail was large, from ten to fifteen letters every day, with all sorts of theses, criticisms, internal polemics, news from Moscow, as well as telegrams about political matters and inquiries about L.D.'s health. Great world problems were mingled with minor local matters that here seemed also so important."

It seemed a prototype for the life later at Coyoacan. "The little low-ceilinged room was crammed with tables spread with manuscripts files, newspapers, books, copied excerpts and clippings." Lyova acted as his secretary. He was to serve Trotsky loyally and passionately till he died.

The G.P.U. was at first amenable to Trotsky, even sending

1. Trotsky in his study

2. Lenin and Trotsky

3. Trotsky as Commissar o
War in 1920

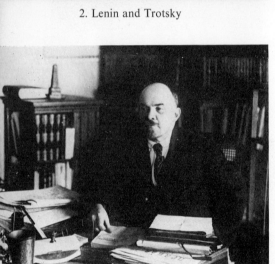

4. Lenin at his desk

5. Stalin

6. The Trotskys arriving in Mexico City, 1937

7. The house at Coyoacan before the fortifications were built up

8 and 9. Robert Sheldon Harte and his guard, Mariano Vasquez. 10. The body of Sheldon Harte. 11. The corner of Trotsky's bedroom after the first assassination attempt

12. Trotsky's study

14. Jacques Mornard
in 1940

13. Trotsky and Natalya with the rabbits

15. Jacques Mornard, alias Ramon Mercader, on the day of the murder . . .

16. and in his cell fifteen years later

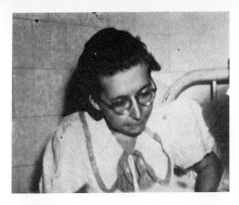

17. Sylvia Agelof on the day she faced Mornard in the hospital

18. Trotsky's study after the assassination

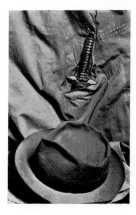

19. Mornard's coat, hat and knife

20. Police chief showing the ice-pick to reporters. 21. Trotsky's body being prepared for lying in state. 22. Trotsky's tomb in the garden at Coyoacan

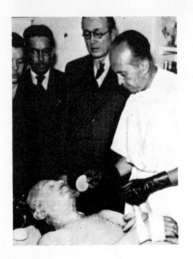

his archives after him in a huge lorry-load. Then in the autumn suddenly communications by letter and telegram ceased. Trotsky's illnesses returned; he suffered from colitis and gout. Natalya wrote to Moscow – "Health can be maintained at a certain level only through a proper regimen and the right sort of treatment. Neither one nor the other is procurable at Alma Ata."

A representative of the G.P.U. turned up at the farmhouse: he handed Trotsky an ultimatum saying that he must stop directing the political opposition. Trotsky replied in a letter to the Central Committee in Moscow saying that this would be "tantamount to renouncing the struggle against a strangling party machine ... tantamount to passively acquiescing in that economic policy of opportunism which is undermining and shaking the foundations of the dictatorship of the proletariat..." The agent of the G.P.U. waited for further instructions. In January 1929 orders came through that Trotsky was to be deported from Russian territory.

Again, he made it clear that he would only suffer this under protest. He was put in a car and towed over a mountain pass in a snowstorm by a tractor; the tractor stuck in the snow; "seven men and a good many horses" died. When they reached the railway Trotsky and his family were put in a train which remained twelve days in a siding. He read Anatole France and a History of Russia in a temperature of 53 degrees below zero. "Grippe raged in our car." The train eventually reached Odessa, where Trotsky had been to school thirty five years before.

He was put on a boat and was told he was going to Turkey. An ice-breaker had to clear a passage through the Black Sea. On arrival at Constantinople he sent a note to the President of Turkey – "I have the honour to inform you that I have arrived at the Turkish frontier not of my own choice and that I will cross this frontier only by submitting to force. I request you, Mr President, to accept my appropriate sentiments. L. Trotsky."

He lived for a while in the Russian Consulate; then he rented a house on the island of Prinkipo in the sea of Marmara – a traditional home for exiles. He moved there in the spring. Here he again enjoyed some "lapses into barbarism"; he spent as much time as he could going out with the local fishermen; he worked in the garden of the large house almost empty of furniture. He now had to earn his living; but for the first time for years he was free to write what he liked and publish it where he liked. Some of his first articles from Prinkipo were bought by the London *Daily Express*. The *Saturday Evening Post* paid him 45,000 dollars for the serialisation rights of his *History of the Russian Revolution*. Trotsky explained – he had no other income, and even Marx had used the capitalist press to keep himself alive as well as to spread propaganda. But Stalinists in Russia could use his literary activities as propaganda against him. What few followers he still had in Russia were exiled or put in prison.

There is some mystery about why Stalin had allowed Trotsky out of Russian territory – why he did not have him imprisoned or killed. Outside Russia Trotsky had some scope in which his powers of persuasion might have influence even if his practical power in Russia had been stifled. But at the end of the 1920's it would have been dangerous for Stalin to try to destroy Trotsky – in this event his myth might grow and might turn to destroy Stalin. There was still an enormous power just in Trotsky's name, both in Russia and in western Europe. Stalin was faced with a country on the brink of counter-revolution: he had to try to keep Trotsky's opposition impotent without resurrecting him as a martyr. And he could always keep an eye on Trotsky even outside Russia – and take more savage precautions when the moment came.

From the time of his stay in Prinkipo the dealings of the G.P.U. with Trotsky lost their quality of sometimes amiable if ruthless farce and take on the lunacy of nightmare. Stalin pursued Trotsky constantly with agents of the G.P.U.: they popped up in his life like grinning skeletons in a Ghost Train.

There was a man called Jack Soble (or Sobel, or Sobolevicius, or Senin) who came to work for Trotsky in Prinkipo in 1931 and who "duly reported back to the Kremlin everything Trotsky told in confidence, including pungent remarks about Stalin". The admission is from Soble himself, who was arrested for spying in 1957 in New York where he was carrying on business as an importer of bristles. But his own evidence about spying on Trotsky in Prinkipo is suspect – Sobel or Sobolevicius had been for years an active Trotskyite in France and Germany; he had helped Trotsky with much of his secret correspondence and had supplied him with material for his books. It seems likely that in Prinkipo he was in two minds – as people so often were who approached Trotsky – and he went as usual to and fro between imagining him a hero and a traitor. Trotsky, again typically, insisted on believing that Soble had been loyal all the time he was working for him though he admitted he was a Stalinist agent later. Trotsky met Soble again in Copenhagen where he had been allowed to go from Prinkipo to lecture in 1932: this meeting was used by Stalin in the purge-trials later to prove that Trotsky was actively plotting against Russia. Trotsky's version of the meeting was – "I had the suspicion that the so-called Trotskyite was more or less an agent of the Stalinists. He came to assure me that it was not true – that is, Senin came, and we had a conversation. . . ." Soble's or Senin's version was – "Trotsky called me and in a fit of rage told me he had discovered what I was up to. He said – 'You will one day regret what you are doing. I never want to see you again!' "

In this twilight world of no accepted framework of loyalties but of men still obsessed with the mechanisms of power there was no knowing who was a spy, a double spy or treble spy, or who was an *agent-provocateur* – there was no knowing this either by the victims or often by the agents themselves – it was as if by losing a customary frame of reference they had lost some bearings in their minds. Betrayal and deceit had become a way of life: they took what jobs were going in their profession. Many of those who had once been Trotskyites and then had spied on Trotsky were much later arrested in the United States. Soble tried to kill himself in 1957 by swallowing "one pound nine ounces of nuts and bolts" in Lewisburg Penetentiary.

In 1934 a man called Zborowski appeared in Trotsky's entourage. He was a student who had studied medicine and philosophy at the universities of Rouen and Grenoble. Trotsky was by this time staying in France (the story of the stalking of Trotsky by the G.P.U. runs parallel to, though fundamentally is separate from, the more important political life of the quarry): Zborowski became the great friend of Trotsky's son Lyova. When Trotsky left France for Norway Lyova was left in charge of the Trotskyite organisation in Paris; his right-hand man was Zborowski. Zborowski had access to all important documents including underground information from Russia. Zborowski was an agent of the G.P.U. and was passing the information back to Stalin. This information was used in the purge-trials of the later thirties. At the founding conference of Trotsky's Fourth International in Paris Zborowski was given by Lyova the task of welcoming the delegates who were supposed to be travelling incognito to keep their identities from Stalin. Trotsky later gave Zborowski a signed photograph for his services.

All this came to a head in the matter of Trotsky's archives, which had been carried by him to Paris all the way from Alma Ata. Lyova knew that the G.P.U. wanted to get hold of the archives. He asked Zborowski to pack them and take them for safe keeping to the International Institute of Social History where he, Zborowski, worked. Zborowski did this. Zborowski then had to break into his place of employment, the International Institute, in order to steal the archives for the G.P.U. He took only part of them – which perhaps shows some recognition of ambivalence.

There was an outcrop of political murders and abductions at this time – a G.P.U. official, Ignace Reiss, defected and was found shot on a road near Lausanne – he had been on his way to make contacts with Trotskyites in Paris. One of Trotsky's secretaries, Erwin Wolf, was deported from Norway and went to Spain where he was murdered. Another defector from the G.P.U., Krivitsky, was pursued by Stalinist agents who had been put on his track by Zborowski and went to Lyova in Paris and was given as a bodyguard – Zborowski. He was found shot in a hotel room in Washington in 1941.

At the back of much of this mayhem there was, or was said to be, General Kotov or Leonid Eitigon – Caridad Mercader's lover. General Kotov was in Spain organising his schools for saboteurs – to one of which he had sent Caridad's son Ramon. General Kotov was said at this time to be trying to change his appearance – he grew a beard and a moustache – but he found that he was then instantly recognisable as a famous guerilla leader called General Campesino.

The Zborowski story resulted in a tragedy for Trotsky. In 1938, when Trotsky was in Mexico, his son Lyova, still in Paris, became ill. He was rushed to hospital by Zborowski. The hospital was run by White Russian *émigré* doctors, obviously hostile to Trotsky. Lyova had an abdominal operation: he seemed to be recovering; then a few days later he was found wandering delirious in the corridors. He died. Years later, agents of the G.P.U. under arrest admitted that he had been poisoned.

Trotsky, in Mexico, was distraught. He had often been bullying with Lyova, but he depended on him deeply. Trotsky and Natalya locked themselves in their bedroom for several days. Trotsky wrote a lament for Lyova – "It might appear that our relationship was marked by a certain severity and estrangement; but underneath there lived a deep, a burning mutual attachment, springing from something infinitely greater than blood kinship – from commonly held views, from shared sympathies and hates, from joys and sufferings experienced together, and from great hopes cherished in common."

Zborowski came to his own sad end. He was arrested for spying in the United States in 1958 while working as an anthropologist for Columbia and Harvard universities. He and Jack Soble – who had become his superior officer in the G.P.U. – each gave evidence against the other. They were sentenced and imprisoned.

With all this coming and going of traitors and murderers as if in a hellish bedroom farce it should not have been difficult, one would have thought, for a stage-manager such as Leonid Eitigon or General Kotov to have introduced an assassin into Trotsky's entourage at any time: Eitigon was one of the heads of a world-wide organisation with huge resources; Trotsky by this time was almost alone in a suburb of Mexico. But it seems to be one of the pleasures of murderers like that of pornographers to spend as much time as elaborately as possible in preparation for the deed: they lead vacuous lives, and the actual event only takes a few seconds.

There was a man called Louis Budenz, a native of Indiana. He was a G.P.U. agent posing, as usual, as a Trotskyite. In the thirties he was national secretary to The Conference of Progressive Labour Action. In New York he had a colleague called Roberts or Rabinowitz – who was officially the representative of the Soviet Red Cross in the U.S.A.

Budenz and Roberts became friendly with a woman called Ruby Weil, who was a Stalinist. They sent her to one of the secret training schools which seemed to have spread to New York from Moscow via Barcelona. The task for which she had to be specially trained, Budenz told her, was to renew a friendship she had once had with Hilda Agelof, the sister of Sylvia.

Sylvia Agelof was planning to go on a trip to Europe in the summer of 1938. Ruby Weil, having been trained successfully in her task of becoming friendly with Hilda, moved on to Sylvia, and proposed that she should accompany her to Europe. In Paris that summer there was the founding conference of Trotsky's Fourth International. Sylvia and Ruby travelled to France together. Ruby, on the boat, was suspected by Stalinists of having become too friendly with Sylvia and was followed by a shadow called Gertrude. In Paris Ruby introduced Sylvia to the 34 year old Belgian called Jacques Mornard – who turned out to be a friend of Gertrude's.

Sylvia Agelof and Jacques Mornard fell in love. She at least fell in love with him and he, after Trotsky's death, protested that he had loved her. He had anyway to pretend to be in love, and pretences in his world were apt to stand for reality. Jacques and Sylvia went through the motions of lovers in Paris in the spring: he knew about restaurants and night-clubs; he seemed always to have money. The money came from his rich father in Brussels, he said; also from his job, which was that of a sports-writer for newspapers. He did not take Sylvia to any sporting events. She did not take him to her political events, and at first she did not tell him she was a Trotskyite. As a student in New York, she had been trained in psychology. She sometimes left her lover to go to do her job as interpreter for the people arriving incognito for the conference of the Fourth International.

There was another startling murder at this time – a body was found floating on the Seine. Its head and arms and legs had been cut off – by someone, the police said, who must have had a knowledge of anatomy or carving. The body was identified tentatively as that of a man called Klement – who had been secretary to the Fourth International. Klement had disappeared leaving a suitcase in a luggage office from which a number of papers had been stolen. These papers would have been of interest to the G.P.U. The only person who knew of the where-abouts of the suitcase beside Klement, was Zborowski.

Much later, indeed after the murder of Trotsky, people who had known Jacques Mornard in Paris remembered how he used to boast of his strength and his prowess at carving. This might, or might not, have been learned by Mercader during his time as assistant chef at the Barcelona Ritz. Or people's memories might be fantasy.

Jacques Mornard in the summer of 1938 left Paris hurriedly for Brussels. He wrote to Sylvia explaining that his old mother had been injured in a car crash. Then he explained that there would be difficulty in rejoining her in Paris because he was trying to arrange his evasion of the Belgian call-up. Sylvia suggested that she should join him in Belgium, but he explained that his family might not approve of this.

The two were together again in Paris for a time in the autumn, and Sylvia was kept happy. Ramon said that he knew of a publishing company who would take some articles from her on psychology; she could write what she liked and would be paid a retainer of 3,000 francs a month; the only stipulation was that she would not ask to see where the articles were published. He promised that later they would be together in New York and Mexico City.

The Trotskyites in Paris did not seem to have questioned Mornard's stories: in the political atmosphere of the time this perhaps was not surprising. It was not much use to ask anyone in the revolutionary world anything personal; few people felt truth important enough to be able to give a true answer or to judge one. By 1939 the G.P.U. itself was disintegrating as a result of the purges that Stalin was carrying out in Russia. Trotsky, in Mexico, was himself bemused by the multiplicity of betrayals. One of the G.P.U. agents threatened in the purges had been General Orlov – the opener of Mercader's school for saboteurs. General Orlov defected and fled to Mexico. In 1939 he wrote a letter under an assumed name to Trotsky informing him that there was a G.P.U. agent at the centre of the Trotskyite organisation in Paris: he gave a physical description which exactly fitted Zborowski. Trotsky decided to ignore the information on the grounds that it could have been planted on him by an agent-provocateur of the G.P.U.

It was in this sort of atmosphere that Ramon Mercader turned up in Mexico City in 1939. There did not seem much point in anyone asking him who he was or what he was up to. There had been too much bewilderment not only amongst so-called-Trotskyites, but in Stalin's Russia.

Chapter 12

With Trotsky out of the way on Prinkipo Stalin was able to launch his drive for industrialisation and the collectivisation of agriculture. The inevitability of Marxism had broken down – it had been foreseen that there would be a period of upheaval during the overthrow of bourgeois rule by the working class but after this the transition from revolution to full socialism was supposed to take place peacefully. This had not happened. Twelve years after the revolution the state was having to allow farmers certain "capitalist" incentives for any business to be done at all, industrial progress was non-existent, and low-paid workers everywhere were in a state of revolt.

Because faith in Marxism had become for communists a necessary mental structure it could not consciously be admitted that some basic tenet of Marxism might itself be wrong; for such a failure there had to be a scapegoat. And because the point of dogma at which Marxism seemed to have failed was to do with the working class – it had been believed that the working class, when oppression had been removed, would by some sort of grace become altruistic and not suffer from the sins of greed and self-interest that had bedevilled its oppressors – the scapegoat in some sense had to be the workers: to the Bolshevik rulers they were the god that had failed; the rulers had no means of admitting faults among themselves.

The working-class became something of a scapegoat even to Trotsky. In Mexico he wrote of the possible "congenital incapacity of the proletariat to become a ruling class": but at the same time he, alone of the old Bolsheviks, had enough wisdom to see that there might be another role for the class-struggle and

105

for revolution – indeed for his own idea of permanent revolution. This would not depend on the expectation or demand that there could ever be a perfect status quo – this might indeed be impossible – but rather on an understanding of Marxism which would not be concerned with political dogma but with dialectics; this might be more to do with a revolution in the mind, but still by this, in Trotsky's sense, humanity could be kept moving.

With the failure of the old conception of Marxism and with Trotsky in exile most of the people who in the twenties had fought with Trotsky in Russia now recanted and made their peace with Stalin. If there was to be a scapegoat, they did not want to miss the sacrifice.

Only Trotsky remained actively in opposition from outside. He himself was a scapegoat: and to incapacitate him further, Stalin had stolen many of his ideas.

Trotsky had advocated industrialisation and collectivisation of agriculture but had insisted that these could be achieved peacefully. But he had said this in opposition where it is easy as well as a duty to condemn the use of force. The story of Stalin's enforced socialisation of Russia in 1930 is one that is difficult for the mind to dwell on – not only because there are so few records, but because of the magnitude of the achievement as well as the cost. By the end of the year, Stalin claimed, about half the farms in the country – 13 million – had been collectivised: peasants clinging to their private rights had been driven from their land; they had been forced to pool their resources and accept new methods of production or else they were deported to Siberia. The forces used against them were small, well-trained bands from Moscow who would arrive in a village and set about the business of persuasion: the peasants were taken by surprise and were usually too sluggish to fight back; or when they did, they fought only in wrecking skirmishes. The men against them carried machine guns. It is about the number of the victims that there is little evidence; what was apparent was the operation's success. During the Second World War, when Stalin was asked by

Churchill whether the revolution had been as hard a time for him as the enforced collectivisation, Stalin replied – "Oh no! the Collective Farm policy was a terrible struggle!" and added, raising the fingers of two hands, "Ten millions! Four years it lasted!" But by the time of the turning-point of the war in 1943 there was hard evidence of the policy's success – for which his democratic allies were presumably grateful. In 1930 there was the beginning of the brutality by which Stalin transformed Russia into the country which could, and did, defeat Nazi Germany. Stalin began at the bottom where, as an orthodox Marxist, he believed the real power lay: and continued to the top, where in ghastly ritual the later scapegoats could be made public.

Trotsky's answer to all this from his Levantine island was to utter his cries of protest – not against the policy, for he had known that in Russia socialism would have for a time at least to be imposed from the top – but against the methods. He argued – If only this situation had been seen before, it could have been dealt with more gently and more slowly. But he seemed to see something of Stalin's predicament too – with Russia on the edge of counter-revolution he discouraged what few followers he had left from plotting any violence against Stalin. Trotsky often found his feelings, if not his mind, split by Stalinism: it was as if he knew emotionally at moments that Stalin might be a necessary force for the defeat of counter-revolution and the salvation of the workers' state; just as it was necessary for him, Trotsky, and with the same aims in mind, to pour out protests from a distance about the means by which this was achieved.

It was now that the two men seemed to take on their somewhat mythical rôles – Stalin the man in solitary power and cursed with the commitments of power – the apparent necessity, in the ordering or progress of human affairs, for some violence and deceit: and Trotsky out of power, straightforward and advocating reason, but also with the ability to glimpse even if almost unconsciously the necessity of paradox, and by just this glimpse perhaps to achieve some synthesis. Both men claimed that they believed in dialectics – the way in which life moves by one state of affairs being presented by its opposite and by just this confrontation there being created a further outcome. And Trotsky at least seemed to understand what this meant. But still, by the two men in the heat of the struggle such a concept as synthesis could hardly be admitted. And other figures were silenced or dispersed – even statesmen in other countries did not seem to notice what was happening. Stalin's enormities were outside their experience; they were outside everyone's experience – except perhaps Trotsky's. He, after all, had led the Revolution; created the Red Army. Each man helped to build up the other's myth – Trotsky built up Stalin's rôle as monster by his invective: Stalin built up Trotsky's rôle as wrecker by his need for a further scapegoat – a scapegoat for making a scapegoat of the working class. It could be thought even that Stalin might have allowed Trotsky to stay alive during the 1930's because he needed this scapegoat for the disasters in his country for which he could say that Trotsky was responsible. From Prinkipo, Trotsky was held to be responsible for sabotage in factories, disruption of agriculture, all the miseries of Russia – and people would believe this because they too needed a myth. It could be thought even that by his vision in exile Trotsky kept some worthwhile part of Stalinism alive; because without his insistence on sanity some life-force of Marxism might have become battered beyond resurrection.

The mass executions, purges, deportations began with the enforcement of collectivisation and became then almost a habit; there had always been cruelty together with apathy in Russia, but with the emergence of the trained political police – the organised and organisational gangster – violence and humiliation became a way of life. A man in the grip of this sort of set-up could always say he was acting under orders, or believe he was acted upon by orders, and that these orders were magically authorised by history – and against this there could be no appeal. Because everyone believed in the way history was going but no one could tell which way in fact history was going anyone could make out it was going any way he wished – and in this atmosphere each man fought for himself – so perhaps it was as well to betray your neighbour quickly before he had the chance to betray you. The only observable mechanism of trust was the party machine – trust meant becoming and staying part of it – men seemed to have turned into the components of a machine. The result of arbitrariness and terror was the death of the mind and heart.

The peasants in Russia were herded into barracks – whether to farm collectively or to die in Siberia. Their efforts at protest were purely destructive – they were said to have slaughtered, in a few months, forty million goats and sheep, fifteen million cattle, seven million pigs and four million horses – and mostly ate them, before the police had time to take them away. They brewed vodka, remained drunk for weeks, and set fire to barns and stables. The collectivisers used their machine-guns. Both sides were in a moral void in which destruction was the only activity because it was arbitrary; that which is not destructive has to be nurtured and to grow.

Trotsky suffered something of this atmosphere in his own private life. One of his daughters by his first marriage, Nina, died of consumption in 1929; she was in Moscow and he could not visit her. His other daughter, Zina, managed to join him for a time with her son Seva in Prinkipo – both his sons-in-law had disappeared in purges – and for a time Zina showed a passionate attachment to Trotsky, and then she quarrelled with his son Lyova, who was also devoted, and she appeared to be losing her reason. Trotsky found it difficult to live with Zina: he quarrelled with Lyova: perhaps he too needed a scapegoat. Both Zina and Lyova left for Berlin, where later Zina killed herself. She had been under psychoanalytic treatment and had cried out against the "filth of her unconscious". In a last letter to Trotsky she wrote – "Instinct has terribly keen eyes which see in the dark . . . what is more frightful is that it hits infallibly and mercilessly those who are in its way. . . . Do you know what has sustained me? *Faith in you.* . . . And this is not instinct."

Trotsky poured out his letters, tracts, pamphlets. He offered advice to Russia, Spain, Great Britain, Germany. He prophesied the rise of Fascism unless there was a united front of socialists to stop it: he glimpsed the future battleground in Spain. He wrote – "For the very reason that it fell to my lot to take part in great events, my past now cuts me off from chances of action. I am reduced to interpreting events and trying to foresee their future course." But he wrote two enormous books about the past – his *Autobiography*, and the three volumes of the *History of the Russian Revolution*. These are works of some genius; of a man with a marvellous literary eye and style.

The *Autobiography* is the best book for a reader to get to know Trotsky – at least, the most sympathetic. Trotsky's descriptions of his childhood are as lively as any in literature. The whole story, which goes up to the time of Prinkipo, pulsates with enthusiasm – even if at the end this is flagging. It is Trotsky's vast energy which, even through his pride, gives him humility. In the *Autobiography* he was dealing with facts: the humility is often lost in his polemics. Yet Natalya wrote of his writing the *Autobiography* in Prinkipo – "It was very difficult for L.D. psychologically to enter into this work. It was so sharply out of harmony with the general bent of his being. He had to force himself to 'recollect'. This reacted on his nerves and his health on the whole became impaired."

The *History of the Russian Revolution* is a prodigious work which describes detailed events at a turning point in history through the eyes and mind of a leading participant. As such it is unique. It teems with the fever, the blood, the urgency of revolution. The chapter on the storming of the Winter Palace for instance maintains the impression that here some fate of the world hung; yet it contains convincing touches of minuscule human farce. This was the irony, as Trotsky had said in his Introduction, "deep laid in the very relations of life". The whole struggle is seen as movements like those of cells under a microscope – surging and apparently random but in fact not – because there were one or two almost hidden influences that were decisive, and the outcome was an organism that was growing.

In Russia Stalin was beginning to organise his own presentation of history which would describe in grim official prose a Revolution in which Trotsky had never existed.

Trotsky left Prinkipo only once in three and a half years – to deliver his lecture in Copenhagen. He was granted temporary visas and went by boat to Marseilles; he was rushed across France as if he carried the plague. In Copenhagen he had his meeting with Soble or Senin or Sobolevicius – during which time he was supposed to have plotted his own counter-revolution against Stalin. Here he had arranged, Stalin said, to assassinate the Russian leaders, poison the Russian workers, and blow up the Russian state.

This was the time when Hitler was coming to power in Germany: politically the old democracies as well as habits of thought seemed to be crumbling. The machine-like men seemed to be triumphing even though in two forces – the Stalinists and the Hitlerites – and only when they had defeated the democracies together did it seem they would get ready to fight a battle between themselves. This would be an Armageddon. Anyone who did not prepare to take sides in preparing for this final battle might seem not to be taking an active part in politics at all – and it was true that the outcome of this battle would be decisive. But the result would not be that which the machine-men of either side had predicted. Trotsky himself wanted Stalin to win: in spite of the violence, the murders, the obscenities against himself, Trotsky felt with his deepest part – his instinct as his daughter Zina would have called it – that Stalin had to win the battle of Armageddon against Hitler or some hope for man let alone for Marxism would die. But if Stalinism won then something else would still vitally be necessary – could perhaps even occur – if he himself, Trotsky, continued from outside to speak against Stalin and to fight him. The ultimate enemy was still the machine-like man: after his victory, he could still be defeated.

111

Chapter 13

Ramon Mercader arrived in New York in September 1939 a few days after the outbreak of war in Europe. He went to see Sylvia and Hilda Agelof in Brooklyn; then he and Sylvia moved to Greenwich Village. He told Sylvia that he had got out of Belgium avoiding the call-up by buying a forged Canadian passport with the name of Frank Jacson. He said he hoped to get a job at the New York World's Fair, and later to go to Mexico where he had been offered a job in a firm of British exporters and importers. Sylvia noticed he seemed to know his way around New York though he said he had never before been there.

The passport with the name of Frank Jacson had been provided for him by the G.P.U. whose practice it was to take over the passports of all volunteers to the International Brigade in Spain and to make use of those whose owners were killed. The Frank Jacson passport originally belonged to a naturalised Canadian called Babich: the G.P.U. procedure was to substitute the photograph and the assumed name and the signature of its agent for those that had originally been on the passport, and to retain the original physical description and date and place of birth. The curious spelling of Jacson instead of Jackson has been held to be a typical accidental mistake of the ruthlessly efficient G.P.U.: it might also have been a double bluff to disarm suspicion, or again simply a decision to use the name Jacson.

Ramon spent a month with Sylvia in New York and then travelled overland to Mexico crossing the frontier at Laredo in October. He gave his address as St Denis Street, Montreal. From Mexico City he wrote to Sylvia to say he was awaiting the arrival of the boss of his export/import firm; and he looked forward to Sylvia joining him. She could not do this at once, she replied, because she had to give notice before leaving her job, which was with the New York City Home Relief Bureau.

In Mexico City Ramon made contact with old friends whom he had known in the schools for saboteurs in Spain. There was Vittorio Cordovilla who had been in charge of liquidating Trotskyites in Calabria; Carlos Contreras, a specialist in executions; Pedro Cheka, who had taken his name from CHEKA – the original G.P.U. Later in the year there arrived Caridad, his mother, and her lover, Eitigon or Eitingon – travelling this time rather lamely under the alias of Leonev.

Ramon had told Sylvia that he had an office in the centre of the city in the Ermita building. He gave her the number of his room. When she came to Mexico later and looked for his office she found that the room number did not exist.

However one office in the building, the police found later, was rented by Siqueiros.

Ramon Mercader spent time in the autumn and winter mountain-climbing. He set off up Mount Popocatepetl carrying full equipment which included an ice-pick. But he became exhausted and had to give up half way.

This was at a time – the outbreak of war – when Stalin had no more use for Trotsky as a scapegoat. The trials and purges of leaders in Russia were over; anyone who could possibly have been a rival to Stalin had been killed. Stalin now faced war – and to deal with this he needed a unified country. And in the aftermath of war, if he won, he would need a unified Marxism to carry into Europe. In both events Trotsky alive would be a powerful enemy. Trotsky himself hoped for a return to power – he had faith in the working class of Europe being bludgeoned to its senses by war and afterwards backing the true socialism which was that of Trotsky. Statesmen in other countries seemed to see some chance of this, even with Trotsky cut off in Mexico. The French Ambassador to Germany, Coulondre, had an interview with Hitler in 1939 and spoke of the turmoil and revolutions that might follow a long war: he reported that he said to Hitler "You are thinking of yourself as victors . . . but have you thought of another possibility, that the victor may be Trotsky?" Hitler jumped up "as if he had been hit in the pit of the stomach" and "screamed" that this was one more reason why France and Britain should not go to war with Germany.

Sylvia Agelof arrived in Mexico in January 1940. She stayed with Jacques Mornard in the Hotel Montejo in the centre of the city. He did not introduce her to any of his Spanish friends, nor tell her of his mother. She took the opportunity of introducing him to her friends the Rosmers, whom she had known in Paris at the time of the founding conference of the Fourth International. The Rosmers were staying at Coyoacan with Trotsky. They took Jacques and Sylvia out to dinner in the town several times. Jacques took the Rosmers sight-seeing in his car.

The Rosmers had come to Mexico bringing with them Seva, Trotsky's grandson by his daughter Zina who had recently died in Berlin. Trotsky had been occupied recently with concern about Seva. Seva's father Platon Volkov had disappeared in the purges, and after Trotsky had left Prinkipo Seva had been brought up in Berlin and Paris by Trotsky's son Lyova and his second wife Jeanne. (Lyova's first wife was at the time threatening suicide in Russia.) After Lyova's death in Paris in 1938 Seva became the victim of a family quarrel which became mixed with a quarrel among rival groups of Trotskyites: Lyova's widow Jeanne had become passionately attached to Seva and wanted to keep him with her; she belonged however to a schismatic group led by her first husband Raymond Molinier. Trotsky himself wanted Seva to join him in Mexico – Seva was now his only direct descendent – his younger son Sergei had also disappeared in the purges. In his wish to have Seva with him Trotsky was backed by the orthodox Trotskyites in Paris. They and the schismatic group carried on a violent tug-of-war: there was a lawsuit during which Jeanne claimed that Trotsky had no legal right to Seva because his first as well as his second marriage had not been validated: Trotsky had to disprove this, and was granted custody. Then Jeanne abducted Seva and hid him in the Vosges from where, with Jeanne suffering from breakdown, he was rescued by the orthodox Trotskyites. Trotsky wrote to the twelve year old boy explaining why he was being brought to Coyoacan. "You are a big boy now, and so I want to talk to you about something that is of great importance, the ideas that were and are common to your mother and father, to your uncle Leon, and to me and Natalya. I greatly desire to explain it to you personally the high value of these ideas and purposes, for the sake of which our family . . . has suffered and is suffering so much."

Sylvia Agelof returned to New York in March 1940. She could not stay too long away from her responsible job with the City Home Relief Bureau. She made Jacques promise that while she was away he would not go to the house at Coyoacan. She said that the matter of his false passport might be an embarrassment to Trotsky.

In May Ramon was living in a holiday camp in the middle of Mexico City which catered for rich American tourists. He would drive off at weekends in a new Buick and return with his clothes muddy: it was as if he had been practising climbing mountains with his ice-pick, or spending the weekend at a farmhouse in deserted country with hills. He would receive a lot of business calls on the telephone. The proprietor of the holiday camp remembered that whenever he spoke on the telephone he would stand with his back against a wall. He kept a heavy trunk and two suitcases in the camp office.

He wrote to Sylvia to say that he had had to break his promise about not going to Coyoacan. Alfred Rosmer had been taken ill, and Jacques had thought he could be useful by driving him to and from the hospital. So he had gone to the house, but he had not met Trotsky.

On the night of 23rd–24th May the holiday-camp proprietor remembered some men coming to talk to Ramon. They borrowed his car, and took away the trunk and two suitcases.

It was shortly after the failure of the first assassination attempt on 24th May that Ramon made his first personal contact with Trotsky. Up to that time, presumably, it had not been known whether this would be necessary.

The Rosmers were due to leave by boat from Vera Cruz to the United States. Ramon offered his services as chauffeur. He said that he had to go to Vera Cruz anyway on business. The Rosmers accepted his offer. On 28th May Ramon drove to the house at Coyoacan to pick them up. He was let in through the garage door where, four days earlier, the raiders had been let in by Sheldon Harte.

There was evidence, later, that Ramon had been an acquaintance of Sheldon Harte in Mexico City.

The garden at Coyoacan is green and shaded with hedges and muddy paths and shrubs and eucalyptus trees. It is more like the garden of a farmhouse than a flower garden, though there is one façade and corner of the house with ornate mouldings and trained creepers like those of a more elegant establishment. Along a far wall are the hutches were Trotsky once kept his chickens and rabbits. By the door from the garage to the garden is the plaque to the memory of Sheldon Harte. In the middle, today, is Trotsky's huge tombstone.

On 28th May when Trotsky saw the man he knew as Frank Jacson come in he was tending his chickens and rabbits. It was 7.58 in the morning. The exact time is known because the guards were now keeping a check on everyone who went in and out of the house. Trotsky welcomed Jacson and for a time they talked about rabbits. Trotsky said that it was difficult to get the right scientific food; Jacson agreed, saying that without it the rabbits stomachs became distended. Jacson saw Seva, and greeted him, and gave him a present of a toy glider. Seva played with the glider on the lawn where four days earlier the fire bomb had burned. Then Trotsky courteously suggested to Natalya that Jacson should be invited to breakfast. They all sat down, the family and the Rosmers and two of the guards and Jacson. They had coffee. Jacson talked a bit about Paris. He said that he had been a friend of Klement, the murdered secretary to the Fourth International.

The dining room in Trotsky's house is dark and narrow at the top of the T of the house with the windows on to the street bricked up and a long thin table in the middle around which all the family and guests could sit. Along the walls in bookcases are piles and piles of newspapers.

Natalya said she would like to go with Ramon and the Rosmers for the drive to Vera Cruz. Trotsky said he had work to do.

Jacson drove his passengers to the sea. In Vera Cruz it did not strike them as being odd – just as it had not struck Sylvia in New York but in reverse – that Jacson did not seem to know his way about the city though he had said that on business he had been there many times before.

Ramon Mercader visited the house at Coyoacan ten times during the summer – sometimes he brought chocolates for Natalya, sometimes he played with Seva, once he offered to go climbing with Trotsky in the mountains. He began to show interest in politics – though not so much as to cause suspicion. In the dispute that was still raging between orthodox Trotskyites and the break-away faction headed by Burnham and Shachtmann in New York Sylvia was inclined now to argue on the side of the schismatics: but he, Jacson, said he agreed with Trotsky. He began to give an impression that he had been more friendly than had been supposed with Trotskyites both in Paris and New York. He told Trotsky that in Paris, for instance, he had given donations to party funds.

In June he left for New York. He drove to the airport with one of Trotsky's guards and left his car for the use of any of the household while he was away.

In New York it is likely that he received instructions from a man called Gaik Ovakinian who was the head of the G.P.U. in America. Evidence for this was given by Vladimir Petrov, a G.P.U. agent who defected in 1954 in Australia. Petrov claimed to have seen the relevant papers in the Trotsky files in the G.P.U. headquarters in Moscow. Also in the files were detailed photographs of Trotsky's home and garden at this time – of Trotsky having coffee with his guards, of Natalya and Seva, and Trotsky's dog. These must have been taken by someone who had been invited to a meal by Trotsky.

Still no one in Coyoacan enquired too much about Jacson. But he had begun to scatter seeds which might have led to suspicion. He had told Sylvia he was working for the British import/export firm: he told her sister Hilda that he was working for a Belgian. He told Otto, one of Trotky's secretaries, that he was a dealer in sugar and oil; he told Joseph Hansen, another secretary, that he dealt in diamonds. To the proprietor of his holiday-camp hotel he said that he was a highway engineer sheltering in the city from the summer rains. He seemed to be scattering clues about his false identity almost as if he wished to be discovered.

When he returned from America he admitted to the guards that he had not had time to visit the Trotskyite headquarters in New York. When they asked, with suspicion, why, Jacson replied that he had been too busy during the day "slaving in an office on Wall Street" and in the evenings in dispute with the Agelof sisters in which he had been arguing the orthodox Trotsky line. Trotsky reassured the guards, explaining – in the words of Joe Hansen – "It is true, of course, that he (Jacson) is rather light minded and will probably not become a strong member of the Fourth International. Nevertheless, he can be won over. In order to build the party, we must have confidence that people can be changed."

This was the time, 1940, when Trotsky himself was being called an agent of American Imperialism: a few years earlier, before the Russian-German pact, he had been called an agent of the Nazis: and now Stalin was an ally of the Nazis and was soon to become an ally of American Imperialism. Words and labels meant nothing any more – the reason why there was not much point in asking what a man was, or on what side he was, was that what was said one day might mean the opposite the next. During the last few years the majority of the Bolshevik old guard who had fought for the Revolution with Trotsky had themselves confessed they had been enemies of the Revolution – all the time, they said, they had been working for the Nazis or for Imperialism. Trotsky and his guards could not be expected to see much point in inquiring into a man's allegiance. Trust had become obliterated. There was left just will – decision – however arbitrary. In Trotsky's case this was just to go on fighting to change the world. For this it was true he could not be too particular in his choice of the people that were left to him to persuade. If trust in people was impossible, it was still important that he should continue to trust in his powers of changing this.

Chapter 14

Trotsky had been allowed to move from Prinkipo to France in 1933. He stayed in a villa called "Sea-Spray" near Royan on the Atlantic coast. Here his admirers at last found it easy to visit him. Natalya wrote – "We had from 15–20 visitors a day. L.D. would hold two or three discussions daily. Full of inspiration and seemingly inexhaustible energy, he astonished and gladdened our friends."

But what was he to do? He had looked forward to making personal contact again with political forces in Western Europe; but the Nazis were now in power in Germany and Stalin's Comintern – the international Communist organisation – had done little to stop them. Trotsky's friends came and went at Royan. Natalya wrote – "In his own physical condition there came the alterations of ebb and flow." Trotsky began again to suffer from headaches, fevers and insomnia. He lay in bed and "heard the storming ocean flinging its spray to the windows of his room". Natalya herself had to go for medical treatment to Paris. Trotsky followed her secretly, and stayed outside at Barbizon.

From here he launched his idea for a Fourth International – an organisation of workers throughout the world that would rival Stalin's Comintern. Its aim would be to encourage a new revolution which could eventually challenge Stalin's bureaucracy. The Fourth International influenced left-wing thought and propaganda but as a political organisation it became a framework mainly for intellectuals and outsiders. Its strength moved to America. European workers seemed to prefer the concrete fantasies of Hitlerism or Stalinism.

The French police found Trotsky near Paris in contact with his political friends and moved him away. He went incognito as M. Sedov to a pension near Chamonix which turned out to be a centre for royalists and fascists. Pretending to be in deep mourning, he and Natalya had meals in their room. They were on their own now. Trotsky became for a while introspective; he for once had nothing to write but a diary. He began to think of death – either of assassination or of suicide or of suffering from an incurable disease. He remembered Lenin's quoting Turgeniev – "The greatest vice is to be more than 55 years old."

Natalya watched over him. They went for long walks in the mountains.

By 1935 the French were trying to get him out of the country – his myth was still fearsome even when he was alone – and he was granted asylum in Norway. At first he lived peacefully in a friend's house near Oslo. He began a new book – *The Revolution Betrayed*. He tried to sort out the quarrels among Trotskyites. He took out some of his difficulties on Lyova, who had stayed behind in Paris to run the affairs of the embryonic Fourth International. He went into hospital for a check-up about his headaches and fevers; but the doctors said there was nothing physically wrong.

The Revolution Betrayed is Trotsky's indictment of bureaucracy. Trotsky saw that even in a socialist state there would grow inevitably some sort of differentiation in privileges; but the answer to this was in his idea of recurring or "permanent" revolution by which the buds of a burgeoning bureaucracy would be constantly pruned. This could happen not only by the revolution being spread from one country to another but by therapeutic effects of this in the country of the revolution's origin, Russia. With so much effervescence going on, a bureaucracy would not have time to crystallise. Trotsky insisted that the workers "should" and "must" see this: since it was in their own interest to curtail the powers of bureaucracy scientifically they would take the necessary steps. But workers were not scientific. And in the meantime Stalin had apparently seen the threat of an overblown bureaucracy himself and was taking his own savage steps.

Trotsky was on a fishing trip with his friend in a lonely Norwegian fjord in August 1936 when he heard of the first of Stalin's show-piece trials that were to dumbfound left-wing politics during the next three years. Zinoviev, Kamenev, and fourteen other old-guard Bolsheviks had been arrested and were charged with acts of terrorism against the Russian state and collusion with the Nazi Gestapo. Their leader and organiser, it was claimed, was Trotsky – who together with his right-hand man Lyova, in Paris was supposed to be sending instructions and gangs of terrorists from Norway. In the fishing village Trotsky's friend ran to tell him of what he had heard on a crackling radio set. His friend remembered Trotsky exlaiming – "Terrorism? Terrorism? Well, I can understand this charge. But Gestapo? Did you say Gestapo?" He and his friend hurried back to their home and during the next five days sat and listened to the radio.

Zinoviev and Kamenev were standing up in the dock and were themselves saying that they had taken orders from Trotsky and Lyova. Kamenev was saying – "We are sitting here side by side with the agents of foreign secret police departments. . . . We have served fascism, we have organised counter-revolution against socialism. Such has been the path we took, and such is the pit of contemptible treachery into which we have fallen."

Zinoviev was saying – "I am guilty of having been organiser, second only to Trotsky of the Trotsky-Zinovietist bloc, which set itself the aim of assassinating Stalin, Voroshilov, and other leaders. . . . We entered into an alliance with Trotsky. My defective Bolshevism became transformed into anti-Bolshevism, and through Trotskyism it arrived at fascism. Trotskyism is a variety of fascism, and Zinovievism is a variety of Trotskyism."

And Vishinsky, the Public Prosecutor, was yelling – "I join my angry and indignant voice to the rumbling voices of millions

122

. . . I demand that these dogs gone mad should be shot, every one!"

Vishinsky, after the war, was to become Russia's Foreign Minister and representative at the United Nations.

Few people nowadays even bother to ask whether anything said in the Moscow trials of the thirties might be true; it is assumed that all the confessions – there was little evidence presented except the confessions – were false. But at the time it was difficult for people to believe this. The size of the fantasy and deception was so immense; so many people – court officials, clerks and secretaries as well as the prosecutors and their victims – had to be in on the fabrication, to convince themselves somehow that it was not a fabrication, that this did not seem a possible accomplishment if human nature was what it had been thought to be. Much of the incredible confessions was believed, just because not to believe was even more incredible.

It was true that Trotsky during his exile had carried on his correspondence with dissident Communists throughout Europe. This was decked out with some of the trappings of espionage – Lenin's wife Krupskaya had been heating up invisible ink over the gas fire in London in 1905 just as Jack Soble, the ardent Trotskyite turned agent of the G.P.U., had been heating up Trotsky's correspondence in Berlin in 1930 – it is as difficult for revolutionaries as for others to change their habits. Also there is a glamour as well as a lack of identification in things like assumed names and invisible ink: and perhaps the carriers of secret correspondences get carried in the imagination beyond the point which the writers intended. But there is still no evidence of the fantasies of the Moscow trials having relevance to facts. Vladmir Petrov, the G.P.U. defector from Australia who saw the official files on Trotsky in Moscow in 1948, says that in all the mass of documentation there was no trace of the letters from Trotsky and Lyova by which the prosecution claimed in 1936 that Trotsky was making contact with Zinoviev and Kamenev and planning to overthrow Russia.

But in Norway in 1936 Trotsky saw that the enormity o the fabrication would mean that people would have to believe it: he rushed to his own files to put together a detailed refutation. This task was to occupy him for years. But it was like cutting off the heads of a hydra – with no relevance to truth being necessary new heads of accusation could endlessly grow. This was one of the ways in which Stalin's machinery did almost defeat Trotsky: it made him fight uselessly in something of its own terms. Trotsky's own style sometimes became simply abusive. But what else could he do?

He wrote – "History has to be taken as she is; but when she allows herself such extraordinary and filthy outrages one must fight her back with one's fists."

In Norway the government were impressed by Stalin's accusations; they said that by his plots Trotsky had broken the conditions under which he had been allowed into Norway. Trotsky denied the plots, but the government forbade him to publish any denial – they said that this itself would be plotting. The Norwegian government hoped to stay friendly with the Russians. There ensued a stalemate: the Norwegians wanted to expel Trotsky but could not do so because no other country would have him, and the Russians did not ask for his extradition because, under Norwegian law, Trotsky could then have demanded a public hearing and so could have defended himself in court. And no one except Trotsky wanted this. The Norwegian Minister of Justice, Trygve Lie, had special legislation passed through parliament to keep Trotsky under arrest without trial and to prevent his appealing to justice. Trygve Lie was later to become first Secretary General to the United Nations.

In Russia, Vishinsky remarked that Trotsky's silence obviously indicated his guilt.

Lyova in Paris took up his father's defence. Up till now Lyova had been somewhat inarticulate; now, with his father silenced, he found his voice. He published detailed refutations

124

of the charges in the trials. It could be proved that Trotsky had not been in places where he was supposed to have met his fellow-conspirators; that aeroplanes which were supposed to have brought his treacherous messengers had not landed at their stated airfields; that hotels where the plots for terrorism had been hatched in fact did not exist. But Lyova suffered in the confusion. The Bolsheviks now making their confessions and accusations had been his friends and heroes in childhood. And he suspected that his own efforts at gathering evidence and publishing refutations were being tampered with. His secretary was Zborowski.

All the defendants of the first trial, including Trotsky and Lyova in their absence, were found guilty of the charges. Those in Russia were shot.

Stalin's purge-trials continued after Trotsky had been put on a boat by a panicking Norwegian government and sent to Mexico – the only country which offered him asylum. The later trials followed the same pattern as the first: party leaders confessed how for years they had been working against the party; they had been taking orders from Trotsky. In 1937 when seventeen leading Bolsheviks were put on trial Trotsky was accused of having come to a formal agreement with the Emperor of Japan; also of having arranged with Hitler to hand over the Ukraine to Germany. He was responsible, through his wreckers, for disasters in the coal-mines, smashes on the railways, and the poisoning of starving peasants. He had spread his swine-fever among pigs and scattered his nails in butter. This last activity, Vishinsky said, was "so monstrous a crime that, in my opinion, all crimes of the kind pale before it!" Defendants told how they had received their instructions here and there from an ever-present Trotsky who seemed to have flitted from place to place like Peter Pan. The Commander-in-Chief of the Red Army and most of his staff were said to have taken their self-destructive orders from Trotsky: an enormous number of civil servants and finally most of the top officials of the G.P.U.

had been in contact with Trotsky and through him with Hitler: they were shot. After a time, there was hardly anyone who had been in a position of power in the 1920's who was left. But as Trotsky remarked from Mexico – if everyone of any importance in Russia had all the time been working for him, how on earth was it that he had not got power? But by this time politicians in Europe had stopped trying to give straight answers to sensible questions. And people anyway did not ask awkward questions about Stalin, in case they were asked awkward questions about themselves.

The show-trials in Russia were for people at the top; lesser lights were simply extinguished. The figures of Stalin's purges are still not fully known: evidence began to come out of Russia in the 1960's. Within one year in the late 1930's 25,000 officers of the Red Army disappeared: 1,108 out of the 1,966 delegates to the Seventeenth Party Congress; 98 out of the 139 members of the party Central Committee. Most of the victims were just taken and killed by the G.P.U.: the usual method was a pistol-bullet in the back of the head. The few dozen leaders chosen for the show-trials all confessed in court: there were one or two who put up a show of denial for a time, perhaps for the sake of seeming genuine to the assembled reporters, then they too confessed.

Outside the top levels of party and armed forces and civil service the numbers arrested without given reason and without record were immense. It has been estimated that between 1936 and 1940 there were 700,000 immediate executions; in 1937 there were about 1,000,000 people in ordinary jails and about 8,500,000 in camps in northern Siberia. In these camps the death rate was high both from starvation and further executions. An order would simply come through from Moscow to the local G.P.U. – "You are charged with the task of exterminating 10,000 enemies of the people. Report result by signal": and in due course there would be the reply "The following enemies of the people have been shot." The conditions in the camps were appalling. In all, probably about 3,000,000 prisoners died. The man responsible for all this, under Stalin, was the head of the G.P.U. At first this was Yaruda; then he himself was arrested as a "thief and an embezzler" and was shot. Yezhov took over, who was said to enjoy the shooting personally; then he apparently went mad and was shot.

Trotsky in Mexico continued his struggle to refute the charges against himself – he seemed more concerned with this, now, than about the outrages in Russia. A committee of supposedly impartial but inevitably sympathetic people came to Diego Rivera's house under the Chairmanship of John Dewey, the American philosopher, to examine the evidence against him. They declared Trotsky not guilty on all charges. This was supposed to impress the world: the world scarcely listened. Hitler was by this time marching into Austria and Czechoslovakia; General Franco was winning the Spanish Civil War. It was not only political leadership in Russia, it seemed, that was savage. And the workers of the world whom Trotsky had hoped to unite were rushing in sympathy everywhere to put on their nationalistic uniforms.

Out of the almost unimaginable and thus easily forgotten terror of the purges two questions remain: the first, why Stalin thought he had to kill so many people: and the second, why so many of his leading victims publicly said he was right.

The question – Why? – was seen frequently scrawled upon the walls of the prison camps in Siberia: people could not believe what was happening. They thought they lived in a rationalist and materialist world and now for the events that were happening there was no material nor rational explanation. Stalin wanted to maintain his personal power – once a man starts killing he can't stop – these were relevant observations, but of little weight against the size of the events. Stalin seemed to want a country stunned; only in this way would it be obedient. In a nation of hundreds of millions of people he wanted one will – this had always been a hope, though in a different sense, of Marxism. There was to be no dissident voice. But in humanity a certain liveliness is usually irrepressible; so that for obedience a whole society had to be hit over the head until it was as it were leucotomised. And the victims did not seem to blame Stalin; there might have been mistakes, but they were not his. He, either because of his violence or because of people's being stunned by it, continued to appear God-like.

Stalin himself said that he had to prepare the country to fight a war. It is true that in 1930 the country was in chaos and that by 1940, after the millions of deaths by brutality, the country did in fact manage to win a great war: and that the winning of this war – not only in Stalin's terms; not only in Trotsky's terms; probably in the terms of most people – was some sort of historical necessity. The difference between Communism and Nazism, which was defeated, was that for all the brutality of means that they had in common the aim of the one, Communism, seemed to be forward, and the aim of the other, Nazism, seemed to be back: and this difference, though on a knife-edge, was total. For history, the war had to be won. But to say this is to trust some god of history – which is what both Trotsky and Stalin did, though this cannot be materially nor dialectically proven. But it is a profound instinct; about which there is not much else to say, except that it is true, also, that in life, at moments of birth and crisis, perhaps millions have to die for there to be a step of evolution forwards. This does not mean that such events are not monstrous: they are, and were in the 1930's under Stalin.

The question of why so many victims confessed their own guilt was partly a matter of torture – the prisoners were beaten, kept days without sleep, bullied and threatened till their minds were deranged; they were promised that their wives and families would be spared similar terrors only if they confessed – so that they probably wanted to die even if promises to them were usually broken. But in addition to this, the confessions were a matter of communist psychology. Trotsky himself had written

128

in 1924 – "Clearly the Party is always right. . . . We can only be right with and by the Party, for history has provided no other way of being in the right. . . . And if the Party adopts a decision which one or other of us thinks unjust, he will say, just or unjust, it is my Party, and I shall support the consequences of the decision to the end."

It was striking how many of the accused, while disputing details of the accusation against them, yet admitted the general principle of their guilt – as if this principle were more important than the facts.

The accused had believed in Marxism. Marxism had told them that history would go in a certain way, where history had not gone. Marxism had also told them to be logical. The fault for the failure of history was, therefore, first of all the proletariat's: but when the proletariat had been forced to do what history had said it should do but which it had not done of itself and there was still failure, then the fault could only be that of themselves, the leaders. And so, logically, they had to confess this.

So they stood up in dock, as if it were before a court of history, and said that although such and such a detail in the indictment were untrue – they had not, perhaps, in fact, done this or that with Trotsky – nevertheless in logical terms the indictment was obviously true, since there was no other explanation of the historical predicament. Although in practice they were not Trotsky's or Hitler's agents, logically because Hitler and not the Communist Party was in power in Germany and there had for years been chaos in Russia, those responsible had to be Trotsky's and Hitler's agents, because if they were not there was no sense in Marxism. And if there was no sense in this there was nothing – they might as well be dead. Which they were about to be; but at least with their faith in Marxism.

The time of the 1930's is a great monument to death – death was honoured like a machine and it devoured its victims in Russia and in Germany – until the two armies of machine-men did meet in Armageddon and there were another ten or twenty million dead – the figures lose all feeling. Most people moved blindly: Stalin and Trotsky might have sensed their rôles in history. One was the slaughterer: the other was the individual voice. This had to be silenced, but it would outlast the slaughter. This was the dialectic.

Chapter 15

After the assassination Ramon Mercader gave two or three explanations about why he had killed Trotsky. He carried on him a letter which would have been found even if he had been killed.

In the letter he said that he, Jacques Mornard, had been a journalist in Paris in 1938 when he had become an admirer of Trotsky. He had joined the Trotskyite organisation and had given all his energy to the revolutionary movement. He had been encouraged to go to Mexico by an official of the Fourth International: everything was arranged for him – his expenses, forged passport, tickets. He had realised, of course, that all this was being done for some reason other than simple altruism; but he did not ask what special service might be required. In Mexico City he had been told not to introduce himself at Coyoacan for some time: then he had been summoned by Trotsky.

When he found himself face to face with Trotsky, the letter said, he, Mornard, found himself profoundly disillusioned. He had expected a great political leader "directing the struggle of the liberation of the working class": instead he found a "man who wished only to satisfy his desire for vengeance and hatred, and who used the workers' struggle simply as a means of hiding his own paltriness and selfish motives".

Moreover, after he had been with Trotsky on several occasions, the letter continued, Mornard was told at last what was required of him. Trotsky proposed that he should go to Russia and there arrange a series of assassinations – first, that of Stalin. This, Mornard felt, "was contrary to all the principles of a struggle which, until then, had been frank and open": and it "destroyed his faith".

The letter tried to take pot shots at as many birds as possible with this one stone. When Mornard had asked about how he was to get into Russia Trotsky was said to have told him not to worry because he could rely on the support "not only of a great nation" but also on that of "a certain parliamentary committee". This was a reference to the American Dies Committee, which at the time was investigating subversive Stalinist activities in the U.S. and in front of which Trotsky had offered to testify. Mornard said he had also been "distressed to discover the close ties that he (Trotsky) had with certain leaders of capitalist countries", and that he had come to the conclusion "that the Stalinists had not perhaps been so very far from the truth when they accused Trotsky of caring as much about the working class as he did for his undershirt". Moreover he, Mornard, had been "astonished to hear with what distrust he (Trotsky) spoke of the Mexican revolution": yet he had also been not astonished "when one considers that he feels the same hatred for the members of his own party who are not in absolute agreement with him". This implied that Trotsky was involved in hostile activities against not only Russia but Mexico, and was so frightened of members of his own party that it was against them that he was having to fortify his house. The money for the fortifications came, of course, from the consulate of "a certain foreign nation".

Finally, the letter said, Mornard had been driven to think of assassinating Trotsky because "when I told him that I could not go to Russia because I wanted first to get married and that I could go only with my wife, he became upset and told me that I must have nothing more to do with her for I must not get married to someone who 'supports the minority rabble' ": and it was on this account, and for the sake of "the young woman whom I love with all my heart" that he, Mornard, decided to "sacrifice myself by getting rid of this leader of a workers' movement who has done nothing but harm it". He was sure, he said, that "history itself will say that I am right, when they see this bitter enemy of the working class disappear".

The letter was so absurd that it was given hardly momentary credence even by the Mexican authorities who must have become accustomed by this time to being told odd reasons for assassination attempts. It also gave rise to the question of whether Mornard/Mercader could in fact be a ruthlessly trained killer for the G.P.U.: it seemed unlikely that the G.P.U. would arrange for a letter to be written in the style and even with the content of a pulp magazine. Perhaps Mornard after all was just a crank. But this was to misunderstand the aims and functions of the G.P.U. By the time the letter would be made public Mercader's deed would have been done: Trotsky would be dead: after that the job of propaganda was not to talk sense nor to be believable but rather to put out as big a smokescreen as possible which by its very vapourising would distract all serious questions.

When interrogated, Mornard/Mercader added to the mystification. He said that another reason he had killed Trotsky was that Trotsky had threatened to expose him as a Belgian deserter; he felt himself "twisted" in Trotsky's hands "like a piece of paper". Further tasks which Trotsky had earmarked for him in Russia were "to demoralise the Red Army", "to sabotage the war factories" and "to assassinate the rest of the Soviet leaders". To assist him in all this Mornard was to be accompanied by a group who had been sent ahead of him, appropriately, to Shanghai – "some by boat, and some by air in the China Clipper". From there they were "to cross Manchukuo and penetrate into the U.S.S.R.".

All this was taken down, recorded and studied not only by the police and those specialising in the criminally insane but by students of politics and newspapers all over the world. Most people neither believed it nor did not believe it – it was good for filling up several inches of space in the press and for filling up several minutes of time by the people who read it. Beyond this, except among people who cared personally about Trotsky, there was little question of belief. In the war there was only the justification, the excuse, the terror.

Mornard took no trouble to make his story sound convincing. When asked about where and when he had written his letter – the police were trying to show it had been written for him or by him at the G.P.U. headquarters in New York – he had a story about buying a typewriter at a stall in Mexico City the day before the assassination and carrying it into the Chapultepec woods and writing the letter on his knees; he had then given the typewriter away the same day to a man called Paris or Perez at a place called the KitKat Club. The police once more could not believe that the G.P.U. would not have provided their agent with a story more convincing. Though Mornard claimed to be the son of a Belgian diplomat and to have been at school in Brussels he knew little about Belgium and the schools he said he had been to didn't exist. When questioned too closely he simply stopped answering. He did not seem concerned. His job had been done. He just had to get through the next twenty years. Nonsense would perhaps be a diversion.

There is an impression at this time that the vital war being fought was not between Stalinists and Trotskyites, Communists and Nazis, nor even between those in totalitarian systems and those in so-called democracies: it was rather, deeply, between forces which seemed to be battering men's minds with random and meaningless assault – and Mornard/Mercader in deeds and words was an archetype of these – and forces which, in spite of this natural tendency to entropy, were still fighting to keep growing some order of mind and spirit. Of these Trotsky was an archetype. With part of him there was the tendency to batter his opponents with any verbiage to hand, but he also stood back and fought for credibility. But the effort to make sense has its own disciplines, and it sometimes carries people where they have not thought they would go. When Trotsky answered Stalin's arbitrary slanders – he was not alive to read Mornard's letter but this was similar in style and content to the confessions at the Moscow trials – he sometimes found himself replying in kind, but he also preserved his voice that was authoritative.

In his closing speech to the Dewey Commission investigating the charges against him in the trials, he said:

"Under an uncontrolled and despotic regime which concentrates in the same hands all the means of economic, political, physical and moral coercion, a juridical trial ceases to be a juridical trial. It is a juridical play, with the rôles prepared in advance. The defendants appear on the scene only after a series of rehearsals which give the director in advance complete assurance that they will not overstep the limits of their rôles. . . . At all the hearings the orators say one and the same thing, taking their cue from the chief orator, in utter disregard of what they themselves said the day before. In the newspapers all the articles expound one and the same directive in the same language. Following the orchestra leaders' baton the historians, the economists, even the statisticians, rearrange the past and the present without any regard for facts, documents, or even the previous editions of their own books. . . . No one acts this way of his own volition; everyone violates his own will. The monolithic character of the judicial trial, in which the accused try to outdo each other in repeating the formulae of the prosecutor, is thus not an exception to the rule, but only the most revolting expression of the totalitarian inquisatorial regime. . . . The play can be performed well or badly, but that is a question of inquisatorial technique and not of justice. . . .

"Democracy is based on the unconfined struggle of classes, of parties, of programmes and ideas. If this struggle be stifled, there then remains only a dead shell, well suited for cloaking a fascist dictatorship. Contemporary jurisprudence is based on the struggle between the prosecution and the defence, a struggle which is conducted in certain judicial forms. Wherever the conflict between parties is stifled by means of extra-judicial violence, the judicial forms, whatever they may be, are only a cover for the inquisition."

Trotsky's defence of democratic processes could not have come to him easily: he had been driven to it the hard way, through his own bitter experience and courage in learning from the facts. For his own "harsh work" in the past, for instance at the time of the Civil War, he repeated that he bore "full responsibility before the world working class and before history": he had "nothing to hide from the people, as today I have nothing to hide from the Commission".

Trotsky's ultimate faith was in life – that truth would work for him if it was allowed to. The faith of his enemy was deathliness – the rigidity of violence and lies. Trotsky's hope did not conflict with what he had always believed about Marxism: "Neither Stalin nor I find ourselves in our present position by accident. But we did not create these positions. Each of us is drawn into this drama as the representative of definite ideas and principles. In their turn the ideas and principles do not fall from the sky but have profound social roots. That is why one must take, not the psychological abstraction of Stalin as a 'man', but his concrete, historical personality as the leader of the Soviet bureaucracy. One can understand the acts of Stalin only by starting from the conditions of existence of the new privileged stratum, greedy for power, greedy for material comforts, apprehensive for its position, fearing the masses, and mortally hating the opposition."

But also – "Fortunately, not everyone can be bought. Otherwise humanity would have rotted away a long time ago." And regarding the Dewey Commission itself – "I did not doubt for one moment that the conscience of the world cannot be bribed, and that it will score, in this case as well, one of its most splendid victories!"

Shortly after this, at Coyoacan, Trotsky wrote his last will and testament. Into this he compressed a statement of his faith which had grown out of so many contradictions. His headaches and fevers had recently returned though the doctors still said there was nothing organically wrong. He had become something of a hypochondriac, though he knew that it was more than sickness that threatened him.

"My high (and still rising) blood pressure is deceiving those near me about my actual condition. I am active and able to work but the outcome is evidently near. These lines will be made public after my death. . . .

"I thank warmly the friends who remained loyal to me through the most difficult hours of my life. I do not name anyone in particular because I cannot name them all. However I consider myself justified in making an exception in the case of my companion Natalya Ivanovna Sedova. In addition to the happiness of being a fighter for the cause of socialism, fate gave me the happiness of being her husband. During the forty years of our life together she remained an inexhaustible source of love, magnamity and tenderness. She underwent great sufferings, especially in the last period of our lives. But I find some comfort in the fact that she also knew days of happiness.

"For forty three years of my conscious life I have remained a revolutionist; for forty two of them I have fought under the banner of Marxism. If I had to begin all over again I would of course try to avoid this or that mistake, but the main course of my life would remain unchanged. I shall die a proletarian revolutionist, a Marxist, a dialectical materialist, and consequently an irreconcilable atheist. My faith in the communist future of mankind is not less ardent, indeed it is firmer today than it was in the days of my youth.

"Natasha has just come up to the window from the courtyard and opened it wider so that the air may enter more freely into my room. I can see the bright green strip of grass beneath the wall, and the clear blue sky above the wall, and sunlight everywhere. Life is beautiful. Let the future generations cleanse it of all evil, oppression and violence and enjoy it to the full."

137

And a few days later, in March 1940, he added:

"The nature of my illness (high and rising blood pressure) is such – as I understand it – that the end must come suddenly, most likely – again, this is my personal hypothesis – through a brain haemorrhage. This is the best possible end I can wish for. It is possible, however, that I am mistaken (I have no desire to read special books on this subject and the physicians naturally will not tell the truth). If the sclerosis should assume a protracted character and I should be threatened with a long drawn-out invalidism (at present I feel, on the contrary, rather a surge of spiritual energy because of the high blood pressure, but this will not last long) then I reserve the right to determine for myself the time of my death. The 'suicide' (if such a term is appropriate in this connection) will not in any respect be an expression of an outburst of despair or hopelessness. Natasha and I said more than once that one may arrive at such a physical condition that it would be better to cut short one's own life, or more correctly, the too slow process of dying. But whatever the circumstances of my death I shall die with unshaken faith in the Communist future. The faith in man and in his future gives me even now such power of resistance as cannot be given by any religion."

L.TR.

Chapter 16

Life continued busily at Coyoacan. Through the summer of 1940 Trotsky poured out his articles, letters, polemics; his reason and vituperation. To people who implored him to go into hiding because they knew another attempt at assassination would be made, he replied that his life would be worthless unless he lived as much as possible in the open. To those who insisted that every visitor should be searched and that a guard be present all the time he was with anyone in his study, he replied that his friends came to him from all over the world often on confidential matters and they could not be subjected to such indignity. The sound of typewriters and dictating machines mingled with the noises of the walls and watchtowers being built up. He wrote in a letter – "We live here, my family and young friends, under the permanent threat of a new 'blitzkreig' assault on the part of the Stalinists and, as in the case of England, the material aid comes from the States." One well-wisher sent him a bullet-proof vest and a siren. Trotsky wrote – "The bullet-proof vest has been piously admired. ... We have not yet decided upon what occasion we will wear it." He allocated it for the use of the sentry on the watchtower. "The siren provoked even more admiration. It is wonderful enough just in appearance. We have not yet tried it out ... for we are told that this siren can be heard from here to Los Angeles. I, personally, consider this an exaggeration."

He was much concerned, though sometimes equivocally, with what should be the correct attitude of Trotskyites to the war in Europe. Some of the schismatic groups in America were saying that now Russia was in alliance with Germany and internally under Stalinism the Soviet Union was no longer a workers' state, there was no rôle for true socialists to play in the war and they should wash their hands of it. Trotsky wrote an Open Letter to Russian workers:

"It is the duty of revolutionaries to defend tooth and nail every position gained by the working class. Against the imperialist foe we will defend the U.S.S.R. with all our might."

To Trotskyites in America he said – "We must of course fight against the war not only 'until the very last moment' but during the war itself. . . . We must however give to our fight against the war its fully revolutionary sense, opposing and pitilessly denouncing pacifism."

And in another letter – "The liberals and democrats say – We must help the democracies by all means except direct military intervention in Europe. Why this stupid and hypocritical limitation? If democracy is to be defended, we should defend it also on European soil; the more so as this is the best way to defend democracy in America. To help England – to crush Hitler – by all means including military intervention, would signify the best way to defend 'American Democracy'. . . . It is the only possibility we have of assuring the defence of civil liberties and other good things in America."

Ramon Mercader returned from New York in July. For a week or two he disappeared; then he telephoned Sylvia Agelof in New York to say that he had been ill in Puebla, in the country south of Mexico City. He urged her to join him.

He went out to Coyoacan to pick up his car, which he had left for the use of the guards. He was asked to stay to tea by the Trotskys. This was the occasion when he told the guards that he had not been to the Trotskyite headquarters in New York, and when the guards seemed surprised Trotsky had calmed their suspicions afterwards by explaining that although Jacson was undoubtedly a political lightweight, they and himself could not be particular about who turned up at Coyoacan to be influenced.

Trotsky was still taken up with laying the blame for the 24th May raid at the door of the Mexican Communists and in vituperation against Stalin. Stalin was "this most malignant of all the Cains that can be found in history . . ." "a syphilis" and "the cancer that must be burned out of the labour movement with a hot iron". Stalinism was "incomparably nearer to cholera than to a false theory".

Ramon Mercader, or Frank Jacson, visited Trotsky's house several times during August. It began to be noticed by Natalya and the guards that he looked increasingly ill. He was pale and sweating – almost green. One of the guards described him "as if some poison were working its way through to the skin."

Trotsky was looking forward to being rid of the business of sorting out the 24th May attempt and to settling down to his "real work" which was his biography of Stalin. The destructive style of Stalinism seemed often to have got under his skin here too; Stalin was monstrous and Trotsky was painting him as such. But Stalin almost alone of contemporary politicians seemed to have achieved something of what he had set out to do. So how could this be explained? There were also passages of dialectical lucidity:

"Stalin represents a phenomenon utterly exceptional. He is neither a thinker, a writer nor an orator. He took possession of power before the masses had learned to distinguish his figure from others during the triumphal processions across Red Square. Stalin took possesion of power not with the aid of personal qualities but with the aid of an impersonal machine. And it was not he who created the machine, but the machine that created him. That machine, with its force and its authority, was the product of the prolonged and heroic struggle of the Bolshevik Party which itself grew out of ideas. The machine was the bearer of the idea before it became an end in itself. Stalin headed the machine from the moment he cut off the umbilical cord that bound it to the idea and it became a thing unto itself. Lenin created the machine through constant association with the masses, if not by oral word, then by printed word; if not directly, then through the medium of his disciples. Stalin did not create the machine but took possession of it. For this, exceptional and special qualities were necessary. But they were not the qualities of the historic initiator, thinker, writer or orator. The machine had grown out of ideas. Stalin's first qualification was a contemptuous attitude towards ideas."

Ramon Mercader, the representative of Stalin in Mexico – specially trained in the "exceptional qualities" necessary to demonstrate the destruction of ideas – began to be so ill that he was not able to get out of bed. He lay for days in his darkened room, as Trotsky sometimes had done. Sylvia Agelof had by this time rejoined him; they were living again in the Hotel Montejo. Sylvia noticed the difference in Jacques: he had always been such a good talker: now he flitted from subject to subject and petered out at a loss for words. He had used to dress smartly; now he stayed half the day in his pyjamas, or when he went out carried an old raincoat over his arm. Once or twice he gave intimations of wanting to kill himself. He was driving along a mountain road one day when he swerved violently to the edge and stopped only just above a precipice. Sylvia did not know what to make of this. She suspected that Jacques might be engaged in some sort of Secret Service work. But nowadays he was professing a great admiration for Trotsky. He used to say – "He has the greatest intellect in the world!"

There must have been several extreme pressures upon Ramon Mercader at this time. He had to maintain a front at Trotsky's household by which he would continue to be welcomed, showing an interest in politics that was neither too ardent nor too amateur to cause suspicion. With Sylvia in the Hotel Montejo he had to keep up the appearance, after two years, of still being in love – a difficult accomplishment even for an actor who had thought himself a bit of a Don Juan. When he went out on business in the town he had to be consistent in his fictions about working for his capitalist bosses: when he met his real bosses in the G.P.U. or the Mexican Communist Party he had to convince them that he was getting on with the job for which he had been trained. And now when he was face to face with Trotsky the reality of killing him might have begun to seem different from the distant prospect: assassinations are done easiest from the anonimity of a crowd in which both victim and perpetrator can seem more of figures than people. Trotsky in his garden or his study was very much a person. And it might have been true that Ramon Mercader had moments of suspecting that after all Trotsky might be "the greatest intellect in the world". Trotsky had his own high view of his powers of persuasion. This was not always misplaced.

Once, when Frank Jacson had been talking in the garden with one of the guards and they had been discussing the fortifications on the walls Jacson had said – "But the G.P.U. will try other methods next time". The guard had said – "What methods?" and Jacson had turned away and shrugged.

Trotsky was under his own pressures at this time – there were analyses to be made about the fall of France, about Russia's renewed pledge of support for Germany, about all the dilemmas of peace and war. He had had faith in the international co-operation of the working class; now he saw workers moving passively to fight in nationalistic wars. He had denounced Russian nationalism; now this seemed the only means of preserving or spreading socialism. He had said that the ends justified the means – but what if the means did not lead to the required ends, or if the required ends did not seem to possess any means? He had begun to feel himself more and more as cast in the rôle of the leader of "the party of irreconcilable opposition": he could protest that the workers "must" do this, history "should" do that; but what if they, and it, didn't? His followers, disgruntled, began to see him opposed to everything – to Stalinism, fascism, democracy, imperialism, the bourgeoisie, religion, mysticism, humanism, even pragmatism. But what was he for? He clung to his pure Marxism; but he did not seem to

143

allow this to be argued, only stated. And this seemed to be in increasing conflict with his practical advice about the war. Trotskyism seemed to have come to mean just the voice of Trotsky – explaining, protesting, scintillating, enduring. This was heroic; but what was the end of heroics in war?

Trotsky worked in the garden at Coyoacan. His chickens clucked, his dictating machines clacked, and pigeons sometimes flew in to set off the alarm bells. His secretary remembered how at this time "He hated pointless conversations, unannounced visits, disappointments or delays. . . . He hoarded the smallest particles of time, the most precious commodity of which life is made." He had with him Natalya, whom he said had been such an "inexhaustible source of love, magnamity and tenderness": and Seva, the grandson of his first wife Sokolovskaya who had written to him a few years before – "I do not believe in life any longer. I do not believe that they (the grandchildren) will grow up. . . . Excuse my cruelty towards you, but you should know everything about our kith and kin."

On 17th August, 1940 Ramon Mercader, or Jacques Mornard, or Frank Jacson, presented himself at the door of the house at Coyoacan and asked if he could see the Old Man, as both Jacson and the guards were used to calling Trotsky. Jacson was carrying his raincoat over his arm, although the weather did not look like rain. And he was wearing a hat, which he did not usually do. He said that he had written an article about the divisions amongst Trotskyites in France, and that Trotsky had said he could come to discuss this with him. Jacson was let in, and went towards Trotsky's study. This was a barely furnished room about fifteen feet square with a long wooden table running away from the window; there were high-backed painted wooden Mexican chairs, a couch, two or three book-cases, and piles and piles of books and newspapers. On the table were the push-button for an alarm bell to the guards outside and a .35 revolver. That afternoon Trotsky had been dictating an article on the theme of the pacifism which he was now constantly denouncing: "There will be revolutionary situations in the coming period. ... At first there will be defeats ... they are inevitable ... but we will learn. ... It is also inevitable we will have victories."

Jacson came up the few steps from the garden. He was still carrying his raincoat and wearing his hat. This was the first time he had been on his own in a room with Trotsky. Trotsky put aside his work and took Jacson's article to read it. He told Natalya afterwards that he had found the article confused and boring. While he was reading, Jacson moved to his side round the table and sat on its edge. This was an unheard-of impertinence. Trotsky was too courteous to remark on it. He suggested a few alterations in the article, and that Jacson should come back when he had made them.

Trotsky sat with his back to the wall which separated the study from the dining room; the window was to his left beyond the table; Jacson was on the edge of the table to his left. The guards were not near them. Natalya was in the town. Throughout the meeting, which took a few minutes, Jacson kept his raincoat over his arm and did not take off his hat.

After the actual assassination it was found that sewn within the lining of Jacson's raincoat was a 13-inch dagger, in a pocket was a *piolet* or ice-pick such as mountain climbers use – this had a sawn off handle a foot long and a 7-inch head with a forked hammer-claw at one end and a sharp point at the other – and in a trouser pocket he had a .45 automatic pistol.

On 17th August, Jacson took his article and left.

Any inquiry into the state of mind of the assassin raises questions inherent in the way in which any history is seen – whether events are the result of the planning of man's intelligence or whether they occur through forces beyond his control: whether men are conscious of their motives or whether they are hidden in distant comprehension. Mercader, or Mornard, or Jacson, had been showing signs of his distress: he had been ill; he had been scattering clues which might explode his false identity. To get confidence for the assassination he might have required a dress rehearsal. Criminals and police, as Trotsky had noted, seem to require settings as if for plays. Or faced with Trotsky alone in his study Jacson might simply have felt, as others had done before him, inadequate. But the form of these alternatives itself begs a question – which is whether an answer is in fact required in terms of either/or. Trotsky with his love of dialectics would not have expected alternatives to be forced like this: he believed in both/and. The assassin, that is, might well at the same time have been carefully rehearsing and yet have found he had lost his nerve. The presence of Trotsky seemed to pose these dilemmas. But only he himself, and not the assassin, would have hoped for a synthesis.

Chapter 17

After his arrest Mercader/Mornard was subjected to what must have been one of the most detailed interrogations in history: he was questioned by policemen, lawyers, sociologists, criminologists and psychiatrists. In the first six months of his imprisonment he spent over 900 hours with psychiatrists alone – six hours a day, six days a week. Since there was no question as to his guilt – he was arrested at the scene of the crime and he had his letter of confession on him – questions could concentrate upon his identity and his motives. The psychiatrists amassed an enormous amount of information about what they thought about him and about what he said he thought about himself; but about his motives, and who he was, they learned almost nothing.

It was soon established that his Jacques Mornard personality was false. There was no Belgian diplomat who fitted the facts he had given about his father, he had not been born in Teheran, and he had got most of his facts wrong about Brussels.

About the question then of who or what he was he managed to concoct a story that made little sense in terms of reality – this was not his job – but which successfully built a fantasy around his activities, which as a G.P.U. agent he was required to do. He could thus satisfy both his questioners and his bosses.

He told of a mythical person who seemed to be a mixture of Mercader and Mornard. In so far as the story had to do with Mercader it seemed to have some relevance to truth – like this it would be easier to remember. (The few facts about the real Mercader have been established independently.) Then when this became too risky, the story could go back to the purely fictitious Mornard.

He was perhaps helped in his task of satisfying his questioners by the nature of psychiatric enquiry – the purpose of which lies in discovering not so much what in fact is the case but what the patient is driven to think is the case; the aim being to expose not history but illusion. In this most patients sometimes find themselves saying what they think the psychiatrist wants to hear; and so their story becomes a fulfilment of the analyst's as well as the patients' desires.

Mornard/Mercader told the psychiatrists that he had had a very difficult childhood. His mother had been unable to breast-feed him and he had been put out to no less than fourteen wet-nurses. But what had kept him alive, he said, had been a mixture of horsemeat and cognac. He had adored his mother. He remembered her as a strong, virile woman who had spent much time riding and hunting. She had often punished him, and would tell him in advance what punishments would be given for what offences. He had accepted the punishments willingly. For instance – once when he had eaten forbidden fruit in the kitchen his mother had come in and found him already standing with his face to the wall. She herself was violently reckless, and used to fall off her horses and crash her motor-cars.

Mornard/Mercader had, he admitted, increasingly identified himself with his mother: as a child when he had been angry he had sometimes kicked against the ground so hard that he had injured himself. Years later when he was examined by prison doctors they found on him a number of scars – on his fingers, his arms, his upper lip, the back of his tongue and his scrotum. He said he had been brutally treated at a school which had been run by Jesuits, to which he had been sent by his father.

He had hated his father who had been a conventional bourgeois obsessed with cleanliness and with fear of disease. He had in fact been so frightened of disease that he had had his vegetables washed in potassium permanganate. Yet Mercader/ Mornard himself was now obsessively clean: he insisted on whitewashing and scrubbing his cell in jail, he asked for a cold shower every day, and he once more dressed meticulously. In sexual matters too, he explained, he had always taken great care not to catch disease.

The one gentle figure in his childhood had been his grandfather, he said – his father's father. This grandfather had used to pretend to go to sleep and had let his grandchildren crawl all over him: they had searched for gold coins in his pockets and had drawn pictures on his bald skull. Another game that Mercader/Mornard remembered as a child was banging nails into the nursery floor with a hammer.

He remembered fighting at school and always trying to prove his bravery. He did exercises to strengthen his muscles. He suffered from stomach swellings and had an umbilical hernia. He had had to be circumcised when he was twenty one.

When asked to describe his mother Mercader/Mornard seemed to be describing himself. She was "tall, slender, green-eyed, muscular, ample hair, light olive complexion, physically agile, interested in sports, interested in revolutionary reading, had had a lot of accidents, has arteriosclerosis; was jovial and cheerful, was educated as a catholic, was amiable and considerate to the servant class, disliked aristocrats".

Her son, the doctors noted, was in addition "mypoic, astigmatic, left-handed and a very heavy smoker". He had abnormally little body-hair and his skin was unusually sensitive. He always seemed willing however to submit to tests which involved pain.

He was also given tests in which, by touch, he managed to distinguish a difference in levels of less than three hundredths of a millimetre. He had a photographic memory. He was given a puzzle consisting of 24 bits of wood with 348 facets: he studied these for three days and then, blindfolded, put the pieces together in ten minutes.

The only test of this sort at which he failed was a puzzle which fitted into the shape of a human head.

For the first month or so of his imprisonment Mornard/Mercader spent most of the time in bed. He would pull the blankets over his head and turn his face to the wall. People who saw him at this time did not know whether or not he was pretending. The question seemed to have no meaning.

This doubt continued when he had recovered. He then became theatrical and at first exaggeratedly charming to people who came to see him; then when faced by difficult questions he would once more become motionless with staring eyes and only his hands trembling; or he would fumble with cigarettes and scatter sparks all over his clothes. Then he would suddenly talk continuously and incoherently again, before withdrawing and pretending to be deaf.

He showed a certain contempt for his psychiatrists. He would laugh and tell them stories about yokels who "could not see further than the points of their own noses". He would sometimes perform a sort of pantomime, playing several parts that they seemed to require of him and putting on different voices. Only when confronted by questions about Sylvia Agelof did his reactions seem to be sincere; then he would weep and still profess violently that he had loved her. After which he would cut off, and show no further interest.

When he was given word-association tests he made a nonsense of them by means of his conventional Marxist training. To the word "commerce" he replied "legal theft"; to "prostitution", "one of the ulcers of capitalist society"; to "Jesuits", "lackeys of the capitalist class". "Trotsky" however, was "a self-centred egotist".

He had a recurring dream. He was swimming in such a way that only his chest and his stomach had contact with the water: the rest of his body could not penetrate it. This sensation was accompanied by a taste of champagne.

When questioned about sexual matters he said that as well

150

as being very careful about avoiding both disease and pregnancy, he liked "slim, nordic women".

He was asked a question about his wrist-watch. He said – "It is my only companion!"

His personal hero, to whom he often referred during questioning, was a man called Kamo, who had been a Bolshevik in the Caucasus in 1907 and who had carried out a bank robbery in order to get party funds. He had fled to Berlin where he had attempted another robbery and there he had been arrested and the Russian government had asked for his extradition. To prevent his being handed over to the Russians and to save his life Kamo had pretended for three years to be insane. He had howled, rolled on the floor, and remained standing in a dungeon for four months. During a hunger-strike he had resisted forced feeding until all his front teeth were broken. He had torn out his hair and arranged it in patterns for his observers; he had lacerated and pretended to hang himself. He had claimed that he had total anaesthesia of the skin; to amuse themselves his jailers had tested this. He had finally been handed over to the Russians because the Germans had become tired of feeding him. But by this time he had established himself as a lunatic, and was saved from execution in Russia by pressure of liberal opinion.

He had later presented himself to Lenin and had eaten almonds with Krupskaya. He had boasted of his revolutionary exploits.

Mercader/Mornard, in Mexico, told his examiners how much he admired Kamo's behaviour. He said – "It is ridiculous for a man to spend his days thinking about what he is going to do! I like to act and to solve my difficulties while I am acting!"

After the 900 hours of analysis the two psychiatrists came up with a 1,359 page report in which they gave the opinion that Mercader/Mornard's psychic difficulties sprang from disturbances in childhood notably with nursing; these had caused emotional insecurity which later grew into an Oedipus Complex

151

of a sort which involved hatred of a weak father and identification with a strong mother. Thus he had become a revolutionary in reaction against paternal authority, and in a social extension of this he had killed Trotsky whom he had cast in the rôle of the wicked father. He had done this for the sake of Stalin who was the ideal father – or, possibly, mother. The G.P.U., in this analysis, might have been some sort of hearth and home. Mercader/Mornard was both narcissistic and self-destructive, the psychiatrists said – "he wanted to sacrifice himself for a great cause and yet at the same time build up an inner world which would protect him. He was weak and at the same time determined; and he showed no remorse."

This might have been an accurate if not very helpful description of many young men at the time. By the 1930's there had been the break-up of patterns of mind that had had something to do with the advent of psychoanalysis as well as the spread of revolutionary politics: the knowledge gained had not had time to settle into disciplined patterns. The blame for a person's ills was often projected on to society. The civilised world with its half-released repressions thus seemed to find itself into a state in which a public blood-letting was inescapable. But for this people wanted an excuse – a rationalisation if not a reason – and they wanted to be given orders which would absolve themselves. The question was asked – is still asked – was Mercader/Mornard in fact the ruthlessly trained killer of the G.P.U. for which there is external evidence, or was he a mixed-up ex-college boy like Sheldon Harte for which there is also the evidence of his behaviour? But these again, as Trotsky would have known, are not necessarily alternatives. It is almost certain, now, that Mornard was Mercader – there is the evidence of fingerprints and of photographs, and the identification has never been denied by anyone responsible. Also it is almost certain that Mercader had his contacts with the G.P.U. from the time when he was sent to the school for saboteurs in Spain to the time when, out of jail in Mexico, he again appeared to be well looked after. But at the same time there is no reason why he should not have been a mixed-up boy – people picked up by the G.P.U. in the 1930's were most often mixed-up boys – there is a mountain of evidence about this in the cases of the knock-about exhibitionists for instance who effectively defected from Britian to Russia in the 1950's. These were drunks; clowns: for a time it could hardly be discovered whether they were working for the G.P.U. or M.I.5 or the C.I.A. – and hardly mattered. They seemed often on the verge of killing themselves: they would not distinguish too much about killing others. And the people who recruited them – those hydras called Eitigon or Valery or Comrade Pablo or General Kotov – they too were probably charming, ruthless killers, and at the same time ninepins sent reeling by the balls of their lack of identity; schoolboys in hotel bedrooms pulling the wings off their own flies. Mercader/Mornard himself perhaps became swept up in a political maelstrom the nature of which he cared about but hardly knew; who agreed to and restored to violence because destruction is the easiest activity by which a bright and lost young man can make his notch in an arbitrary world. Perhaps he felt the emptiness, or the fuzz of verbiage, in his own skull; so that he could best alleviate it by the bashing-in of another. By this the devils could be let out which he had projected into it. The buzzing was like that of mosquitoes; the fever of the world like the malaria that had for so long haunted Trotsky. In the high temperature of the time men seemed to cease to care whether they killed or were killed: the buzzing was inside: outside were millions more mosquitoes.

Chapter 18

On 20th August, 1940 Ramon Mercader left the Hotel Montejo
early. He carried his raincoat over his arm. The sun shone, but
there were clouds above the mountains. He told Sylvia Agelof
that he was going to the United States Embassy to see about a
visa. The two of them planned to go to New York the next day.
Jacques had been ill, and Sylvia wanted to get away from
Mexico. What with the way the war was going and the quarrels
amongst Trotskyites, she felt she had nothing more to do at
Coyoacan.

Jacques returned to the hotel later in the morning. He
seemed in a bad mood. He and Sylvia went out to have lunch.
On the steps of the Palace of Fine Arts they ran into Otto
Scheussler, one of Trotsky's secretaries: he was spending his
day off with his girl-friend in the town. Jacques and Sylvia told
Otto that they were leaving the next day. They were going out
to Coyoacan at tea time, they said, to say goodbye to Trotsky.
Otto suggested that four of them – he and his girl-friend and
Jacques and Sylvia – should meet in the town for dinner at
seven-thirty. Sylvia seemed pleased. Jacques did not answer.
He said he remembered he had another appointment before
lunch, and left them.

Sylvia talked with Otto. She said she was worried about
Jacques; he had been ill so often recently, perhaps it was the
altitude, or the Mexican food. She arranged where to meet
Otto in the evening. Then she went back to her hotel. She stayed
in her room through the afternoon, every now and then asking
the manager of the hotel if there had been any messages for her
from Jacques, but there had not.

Mercader said later that he spent the afternoon wandering about the city. He dropped in at the Wells Fargo Office (a poste restante address) to collect his mail: then he took his car and drove to a piece of wasteland in the suburbs and burned his passport and other papers which would identify him as Frank Jacson. He put the date – 20th August – at the bottom of the typewritten letter which explained his motives as Jacques Mornard for killing Trotsky – the letter which, he said later, he had written in the Chapultepec woods the day before; he signed the latter "Jac" – which could stand either for Jacques or Jacson – then he set out for Coyoacan.

Trotsky had woken early that morning. He had said to Natalya as usual – "Another lucky day! We are still alive!" He said he felt better – better than he had done for a long time. He went out to feed his rabbits and chickens. Natalya brought him a hat to put over his head in the sun.

After breakfast he went into his study. He wrote brief, joking letters to two American Trotskyites who had been in prison for promoting a strike and were about to be released – "It is always preferable to leave rather than to enter such a place!" and – "From my own personal experience I know that such a day is very agreeable." He wrote another letter to an American friend thanking him for the gift of a Dictionary of American Slang – "At meal times I must permanently keep this book in my hands in order to be able to understand the conversation . . . I had hoped to find some abbreviations for the various sciences, philosophical theories, etc.; but instead I found about 25 expressions for an attractive girl." Then he turned to an article which he had dictated two days before on the subject of militarianism and pacifism, the first draft of which had been typed and was on his desk for correction.

His last article is a mixture of analysis and mumbo-jumbo – of an intention to talk authoritatively about the war being waylaid by the temptation to niggle at the Trotskyite factions in New York. He was trying to say that revolutionaries should always be ready to fight; that pacifism was useless; that now more than ever in and after the war there would be chances of revolutionary activity. But the argument got clouded by old ghosts of the past – Mensheviks were still fighting Bolsheviks; there was something called a "Bonapartism" to be opposed to a "pure Bonapartism" and even a "pure Bonapartist Bonapartism". At the end there were the old compaints – if the proletariat had only been different then everything would have been different; it was all the fault of the Comintern, or the Social Democrats, or of labour being so conservative.

At lunch-time his lawyer came to see him about a slanderous story in a Mexican paper about the 24th May raid; Trotsky gave him permission to threaten to sue. He told Natalya he would have to put to one side his article on militarism and the other work to which he had been looking forward for so long; he would again be taken up with local polemics. He said – "I will take the offensive and will charge them with brazen slander!" But he repeated that he felt very well.

After lunch he had his siesta; then returned to his study to work. Natalya, looking in on him from time to time, felt it a day of "physical and spiritual equanimity for him". At five o'clock the two of them had tea. At about twenty past five Natalya came out of the kitchen and saw Trotsky by the rabbit hutches. Beside him was a figure she did not at first recognise.

Joseph Hansen and Charles Cornell, two of the guards, had been working on the roof near the main watchtower when they saw a car arrive driven by Frank Jacson. He turned the car round and left it facing back towards the city. He did not usually do this. Hansen and Cornell were fixing up the siren which had been sent by the well-wisher in America and which Trotsky had said could be heard all the way to Los Angeles. Jacson got out of his car and asked if Sylvia Agelof had arrived. Hansen said she had not. Jacson said that Trotsky was expecting them. Cornell opened the garage door by its electrical controls

156

and Jacson went into the garden. He was received there by another guard, Harold Robins. Trotsky was by the hutches feeding his rabbits.

It was said later that there were two other cars parked near the house at the time; in one was Leonid Eitigon and in the other Caridad, Ramon's mother. They were to help Ramon make his getaway. They were to go with him to the airstrip where a plane was waiting to fly him out of the country. He would be provided with money and papers for a new identity – or lack of identity. But the plan of escape depended on his being able to do his job without making any noise. He might then leave Trotsky dead in his study and be able to get out of the house without anyone knowing or stopping him. Such an assassination had been done before by the G.P.U. – a Russian ambassador in the Middle East had been liquidated thus with an iron bar. Even if there was noise Mercader might still be able to shoot his way out – it was for this, he said later, that had carried his pistol. Alternatively he might shoot himself.

Natalya, when she saw Jacson with Trotsky in the garden, thought he looked so ill that she felt concern. He came over to the kitchen and asked her for a glass of water. She asked him if he would like a cup of tea. He said "No," and pointing to his throat added "I dined late. I feel the food is up here, it is choking me."

Natalya asked him why he was carrying a raincoat and wearing a hat on such a sunny day, and he said – "But it won't last long, it might rain."

Natalya thought of reminding him that he used to boast that he never wore a hat or coat even in the worst weather: but she felt too depressed.

She asked – "How is Sylvia?"

He did not seem to understand. In Natalya's words – 'He seemed lost in his own thoughts.'

Finally he roused himself 'as if from sleep' and said

"Sylvia?" Then – "She is always well!" and he went back towards the rabbits.

Natalya followed him. She asked – "Is your article typed?" She explained how Trotsky did not like reading manuscripts. Jacson pulled the typewritten pages of his article out of his raincoat pocket 'with difficulty'.

Natalya remembered how Trotsky had told her of Jacson's visit three days before; how he had sat on the table and held his raincoat and kept his hat on. She had thought when Trotsky told her this that he, Trotsky, seemed to have 'perceived something new about Jacson'; but he 'was in no hurry to draw' any conclusion.

The three stood by the rabbit hutches. Jacson said that he was leaving the next day with Sylvia for New York. Natalya said that it was a shame she hadn't known earlier, since she might have sent messages with them. Jacson said that he could call in the next day about lunch-time. Natalya said no, this would inconvenience both of them.

Trotsky seemed reluctant to leave the hutches. It was a beautiful day. Jacson's article three days before had bored him.

He suggested to Natalya that Jacson and Sylvia might be asked for supper. Natalya explained that Jacson was feeling ill; he would not even stay for tea.

Trotsky said to Jacson in a tone of 'light reproach' (it was Natalya who remembered all this) "Your health is poor again. You look ill. That's not good."

Trotsky began fastening the doors of the hutches. He did this slowly. He took off his gloves. He always wore gloves when working in the garden because he became upset by scratches, which he thought interfered with his writing. He brushed his clothes. He moved towards the study window accompanied by Jacson. Trotsky wore his blue French peasant's working suit: Jacson wore his hat and carried his raincoat.

They went into the study and closed the french windows. Natalya went into the kitchen. The guards were fixing the siren.

After a time there was a sound such as all those who heard it said they would never forget – a long drawn-out cry between a roar and a scream – an expression both of fury and of pain – so unlike anything else that for a moment no one knew what it was. Joe Hansen thought that a workman must have fallen off the roof; Natalya could not locate the noise. Ramon Mercader himself said afterwards that the cry had "pierced his brain". Hansen looked down from the watchtower and saw through the study window that Trotsky seemed to be fighting with Jacson – attacking him – there was the sound of furniture breaking, of objects being hurled – and Jacson was retreating. Then there was silence.

Natalya rushed into the dining-room and saw Trotsky standing there between the door into his study and the french window. His face was covered with blood. His blue eyes, without spectacles, glittered. Natalya held him in her arms. She thought something must have fallen on his head from the roof.

Trotsky said 'calmly and without indignation' – "Jacson". Then he fell to the floor.

Two guards rushed past into the study where they found Jacson standing limply with his automatic dangling.

Jacson had followed Trotsky into the study. Trotsky had sat at the desk as he had done three days ago. He had had his back to the dining-room with the french-window to his left and slightly to the front. Jacson had again come round the edge of the table to Trotsky's left. He had been carrying – as usual – his raincoat. He had handed Trotsky his article. Then he had put his raincoat on the table. Trotsky had turned with the article to catch the light. Jacson had taken the *piolet* out of the raincoat pocket, had raised it, and brought it down with all his strength on Trotsky's head. Trotsky must have turned to him at the very last moment because from the wound there was evidence that the blow had come from the front.

The *piolet* was the ice-pick with a handle a foot long and the iron head with one sharp end and the other like a hammer or a claw. Mercader had hit Trotsky with the hammer or claw. It went two and three-quarter inches into his skull.

Mercader, with his strength, had thought that Trotsky would make no noise: then he could have joined his mother and her lover.

Trotsky leaped to his feet and began his roar – the sound of which, in Mercader's words: "I will never forget . . . his scream was Aaaa – very long, infinitely long; and it still seems to me as if that scream were piercing my brain!"

Trotsky came towards him sweeping the objects off the table and hurling them at him – the books, the dictating machine, the ink-well, the paper-knife – he grappled with Jacson, tore the ice-pick from him, got hold of his finger and bit it. Jacson screamed. He backed away, knocking over chairs and a bookcase. He gave a push at Trotsky who staggered out of the door. Jacson stayed in the room nursing his bitten finger.

Natalya got Trotsky into the garden and laid him down and put a pillow under his head. She kissed him. He said "Natalya I love you!" Then – "Seva mustn't see this."

The two guards who had run into the study began beating Jacson up. They hit him with their fists and the butts of their pistols. Jacson collapsed and seemed to become unconscious. Hansen hit him so hard he broke a finger.

Trotsky whispered, "Don't let them kill him! He must talk!"

In the study Jacson roused himself and yelled "They made me!" Then – "They've got my mother!"

Hansen came out into the garden and knelt by Trotsky. Trotsky said "Jacson shot me". Hansen said that he thought the wound was superficial. Trotsky held his hands against his heart and said "No, this time they've succeeded".

Jacson, in the study, kept on saying – "Sylvia had nothing to do with this. The G.P.U. had nothing to do with this." The guards stopped beating him. He became more composed. He said "Why don't you kill me?"

160

The police on duty outside had already telephoned for an ambulance. One of the guards ran for the local doctor. He tried to use Jacson's car, but could not find the keys.

Trotsky lay in the sun. Natalya cradled him. He looked towards the window into the study where Jacson lay and said – "You know, in there I thought I understood what he wanted – he wanted to strike once more – but I prevented him!" He said this with triumph.

Ambulances arrived. Natalya tried to stop Trotsky being taken to hospital. She remembered how her son Lyova had been killed in Paris.

Trotsky kept saying – "Take care of Natalya; she has been with me many years."

The guards waited for Trotsky to make a decision about the hospital. After a time he said – "I leave it to you."

When the cortege left Coyoacan there were two ambulances – one for Trotsky with the two and three-quarter inch wound in his skull, and the other for his assassin whom he had bitten on the finger.

Chapter 19

In the hospital there was not much to be done. The pick had done enormous damage to Trotsky's brain. If it had gone in another quarter of an inch death would have been instantaneous.

In the ambulance he had lain with Natalya on one side and his secretary Joe Hansen on the other. He had even then tried to carry out an analysis of the situation – Jacson, he whispered was obviously an agent of the G.P.U.; possibly also of the Gestapo. One of Trotsky's arms was paralysed: the other made circles in the air. It tried to find a resting-place on Natalya.

The streets on the way to the hospital were already filling with people who had heard the news. They watched the police cars and the ambulances rush past.

In the side streets around Coyoacan Leonid Eitigon and Caridad Mercader must have heard the noise, and drove away.

The doctors got Trotsky's skull ready for an operation. He was still talking to Hansen. He said – "Have you got your notebook?" He dictated his last political statement: "I am close to death from the blow of a political assassin. I was struck down in my room. I struggled with him. We had entered – talked about French statistics. He struck me. Please say to our friends – I am sure of the victory – of the Fourth International – Go forward!"

He made this statement in English since Hansen did not understand Russian.

Natalya remained on his other side. When they shaved his head he joked – "You see, I needed a barber!" When they began to cut away his clothes for the operation he said to Natalya

– "I don't want them to undress me. I want you to undress me." These were his last words. He closed his eyes.

Sylvia Agelof had gone to keep her dinner appointment with Otto Schuessler. She was late, because she had been waiting in her hotel room for Jacques Mornard. She had waited all afternoon. She told Otto that she was more worried than ever about Jacques, because he had always let her know if he would be late. He was supposed to have picked her up by tea time, and to have taken her out to see Trotsky.

Otto suggested her telephoning the house at Coyoacan. Sylvia said that Jacques would never have gone there without her. Finally, Otto telephoned.

He and Sylvia took a taxi to Coyoacan. There were now crowds of police and reporters in the house. Trotsky and Jacson had been taken away but the study had been left as it was after the struggle. There was the furniture overturned, the books and papers scattered, the pick-axe with its hammer-and-claw end and its handle still bloody. There was the raincoat which Jacques had so often carried with the pocket now visible where he had hidden the pick-axe and the dagger. There was Jacques' hat, a grey trilby with a black band around it. There were two pools of blood – one from Trotsky and one from Jacson. There were the few pages of Jacson's article on the Fourth International on the floor mixed up with Trotsky's. There was a book that Trotsky had been reading – *Hitler Speaks*, by Hermann Rauschning. The trail of blood led through to the dining-room, where the table had been laid for dinner.

The police watched Sylvia Agelof wandering through the rooms with her small, heart-shaped face with its long nose and gold-rimmed spectacles and short-sighted eyes. She was dressed in white. She looked like a child. She began to weep and yell, insisting that Jacques Mornard should be killed. She cried – "He only used me!"

Ramon Mercader had been taken in his ambulance to the hospital where Trotsky lay dying. On the way the police had read the letter which explained how he, Jacques Mornard, had been a devoted follower of Trotsky's – he had come to Mexico to sit at the Old Man's feet – and then he had become disillusioned when he had been asked to assassinate Stalin. Moreover, the letter said, Trotsky had spoken disparagingly of Sylvia whom he, Mornard, loved with all his heart. So he had decided to kill Trotsky.

In the hospital Mercader's head and one eye were bandaged where the guards had hit him; he sat and chain-smoked cigarettes. He told his story about how he was a Belgian born in Teheran and how he had gone to a Jesuit school in Brussels, and the other details which could almost immediately be disproved. He said that he had decided to use a pick-axe for the assassination because he was accustomed to manipulating it – he "could detach great blocks of ice with it in one or two strokes when climbing snow-covered mountains". He said that he had intended to kill himself afterwards with either the automatic pistol or the dagger in one of the public parks in the city. He said he had felt such a bitter hatred of Trotsky because he felt he, Mornard, was "one of those whom Trotsky had degraded for his own advantage, for without any compunction he forced his own followers to harm themselves for his personal benefit".

Sylvia Agelof was brought to the hospital. She was in hysterics, and was put in a room near Trotsky's and Jacson's. Colonel Salazar was by this time again in charge of investigations: he thought that Sylvia must be an accomplice of Jacson's since it seemed inconceivable that she should have lived with him so long without having any idea of his intentions. Sylvia herself made a statement in which she said that she realised now that Jacques must be an agent of the G.P.U. though she had not known before. "There is no doubt that Jacson is a Stalinist and that behind him are other Stalinists that I do not know. Stalin is the person who has the greatest reason to get rid of Trotsky. And it is I who have served as his tool." She made no effort to defend her lover.

164

Salazar had the idea of bringing Sylvia and Jacson face to face. Jacson was still claiming that it was partly because of love of Sylvia that he had decided to kill Trotsky: at the same time he was protesting that Sylvia had had nothing to do with it. He was told that he was going to be taken to see an oculist for his damaged eye, and was half carried along a passage. Sylvia was lying on a bed in her room with her hands over her face. When Jacson saw her he tried to run. He said to Salazar – "Why have you brought me here?"

Sylvia began screaming – "Kill him! Kill him!"

Salazar explained to Sylvia that Jacson had said that it was out of love of her that he had decided to kill Trotsky.

Sylvia screamed – "Nothing but lies! Lies!"

Jacson said – "Take me away!"

Salazar said to Sylvia – "What do you think of him?"

Sylvia spat in Jacques' face.

Salazar discovered something from the interview: in his pleas to the police it became apparent that Mornard/Jacson spoke and understood Spanish.

Mornard/Mercader was interrogated by Salazar for five days. There were a lot of questions to be asked about routine details such as where he had bought the dagger and the typewriter he had taken into Chapultepec Woods. Sometimes Jacson gave matter-of-fact answers about the man called Paris or Perez and the KitKat Club; then when the questions became difficult he would collapse; then he would sit up again and light a cigarette and smile. Towards the end of the police questioning he seemed to become bored and simply answered – "I don't remember. I don't remember." Salazar concluded that he was "a consumate actor".

Trotsky lived for twenty-four hours after the operation. Natalya and his secretaries stayed with him through the night. He did not recover consciousness. Sometimes Natalya embraced him and he seemed to respond.

Journalists by this time had gathered at the hospital from

165

all over Mexico. They tried to force their way into the operating theatre and into Trotsky's bedroom. One reporter called Blond Telley bribed a stretcher-bearer and carried Trotsky to and fro. There are photographs of the operating theatre – a crowd round Trotsky's head aware of the camera.

The next day, 21st August, Trotsky's breathing alternated between violence and gentleness. By midday there was an improvement: then in the evening his breathing got faster and faster. Natalya tried to lift his head. It drooped on her shoulder. His breathing stopped. He looked, as Natalya herself described the scene, like the central figure in Titian's *Descent From the Cross*.

Salazar made the announcement of Trotsky's death to the reporters. There was a wild scramble for telephones in which two got smashed.

Outside in the city the street-musicians began to sing their *Gran Corrido de Leon Trotsky* – a ballad such as they were accustomed to make up to commemorate a great event.

> Finally destiny has conquered
> In his own home
> Where the cowardly assassin
> Snatched life from him.
>
> An Alpine ice-axe
> This assassin carried
> And being alone with Trotsky
> He attacked him without running any risk.
>
> It was on a Tuesday in the afternoon
> This fatal tragedy
> Which has moved the country
> And all the capital.

Trotsky lay in state for five days in the principal hall of the mortuary. He was on a bier with one of his guards or a Mexican follower at each corner and a banner above him proclaiming his

Fourth International. A crowd of about 300,000 people filed past.

There was a short notice in the Moscow *Pravda* saying that Trotsky had been murdered by a disillusioned follower.

The murder was front-page news in most of the world's newspapers. The stories varied from the assassin being a disgruntled Trotskyite to the likelihood of his being a Stalinist. But in Europe the news was apt to take second place to stories about the Battle of Britain, which on 21st August reached its climax with an R.A.F. claim of 200 German planes being shot down.

The Mexican Communist Party expressed its regret for the assassination but explained how it must have been done by an *agent provocateur*.

A telegram to the press from Siqueiros, still in hiding, expressed his regret for the Mexican Communist Party's regret, and explained that he was only waiting for confirmation of Trotsky's death to come out of hiding.

At the autopsy it was discovered that Trotsky's brain was of unusually large size; also his heart.

Trotsky's body was cremated and his ashes were buried in the garden at Coyoacan. Above them is just a huge pale stone with the name Leon Trotsky, and a hammer and sickle like a claw.

Chapter 20

Ramon Mercader was not brought to trial until the spring of 1942. It was before this that he was questioned for 900 hours by psychiatrists: they had to make a report on his personality for the judge. Shortly after the assassination there was also a macabre reconstruction of the crime such as are supposedly loved by detectives – Jacson/Mornard was taken back to the study where everything was still as it had been on the day of the murder and seals were removed from the door and dust-sheets were taken off the furniture and a policeman sat at the table where Trotsky had sat and Mornard went through his motions with a rolled-up newspaper. But he happened to step on a pool of dried blood and suffered from nervous convulsions.

For a time Mornard/Mercader stuck to the story that his reasons for killing Trotsky had been that Trotsky had confronted him with the alternatives of either assassinating Stalin or being returned to his own country, Belgium, to face execution as a draft-dodger. But by 1942 Russia was no longer an ally of Germany's and hostile to America but, in the switch of the war, an ally of America's and an enemy of Germany's; so that Trotsky, in Mornard's story, could no longer be a secret agent of American imperialism but had to revert to being an agent of the Nazi Gestapo. This alteration was made in Mornard's deposition.

Mercader began to hope that he might even get off with a light sentence. By 1942 Siqueiros and most of the others involved in the 24th May raid were free – Russia's alliance with America had been reflected in public and government opinion in Mexico. So Mercader changed his plea from guilty to self-defence – he said that he had called on Trotsky with his article analysing the quarrels amongst Trotskyites and Trotsky had suddenly attacked him shouting – "You are nothing but a military idiot!" This, Mornard said, was more than he could bear; so he had defended himself with an ice-pick which he had happened to have on him at the time, as also an automatic and a dagger. But even Mornard couldn't think of a random reason for his letter of confession.

He was found guilty. Sentence was not passed for another year. There were still questions of psychiatry – and diplomacy. But it was in the interest of no one now that Mercader should be treated leniently or go free. The prosecution had asked for the maximum sentences under Mexican law – twenty years for premeditated murder, two for assault with weapons, and one for illegal possession of arms. At this time there was no death penalty in Mexico for homicide. On 17th April, 1943 the court sentenced Jacson/Mornard to nineteen years and six months for premeditated murder and six months for illegal possession of arms. The proceedings in court were broadcast, and when Mercader heard the sentence he threw his hat over the microphone in a fit of pique.

Mercader spent the first eighteen years of his imprisonment in the Federal Penitentiary on the outskirts of Mexico City. He had a roomy and sunny cell with a small patio. He read a lot of books and played cards and dominoes with other prisoners. He worked in the prison workshop making toys. His behaviour was so exemplary that he was put in charge of the work. He joined with enthusiasm in an anti-illiteracy campaign and became a "national champion" at teaching illiterate prisoners to read. He had hoped by this to gain some sort of pardon or remission of sentence: he was given a diploma. He became interested in painting, and after a time took up radio and television repair work. He studied electrical engineering, became an expert, and was put in charge of the whole electrical system of the prison.

169

Photographs of Mornard/Mercader in Mexico show, first, the neat and affable European of indeterminate age such as was in his forged passport above the name of Frank Jacson; here there are just the thin spectacles and the diagramatic lines of an identikit picture. Then there are the photographs just after the assassination of the collapsed and doom-laden boy with a long Mediterranean face and the bandage round his head: he looks much younger here, and seems almost to have gained some identity. Then there is a nondescript middle-aged man again with a mop and pail at the door of his cell; solid, bespectacled, once more smiling and indeterminate.

Prisoners in Mexico are allowed to have women in their cells and Mercader had a girl-friend who worked in a night club and brought him food and carried messages. For some time he would not eat the prison food because he thought it might be poisoned: he was in fact sent a box of poisoned chocolates by a supposed admirer. There were grounds at first for his fearing a retributory attack by Trotskyite prisoners, but then life settled down and people seemed to take him for granted.

Sylvia Agelof returned to America in a state of nervous collapse. She has refused to speak of the past. When Mercader was told news of her, he continued to show distress.

There were rumours from time to time of attempts to rescue him. His mother Caridad had gone to Moscow when she had heard that the assassination had been successful and she had received there from Stalin the Order of Lenin. She was also given the Order of the Hero of the Soviet Union to keep for her son.

Stories of supposed rescue attempts belong again to the secret world of double- and treble-agents in which no one knows if anyone is lying and there is no certainty who anyone is. Caridad Mercader was said to have spoken to a friend in Moscow in 1943; she had become disillusioned and spoke of Russia as "the most terrible of hells"; yet she still wore the Order of Lenin "proudly on her chest". She herself wanted to get out of Russia

170

– but she said she was being kept there as a hostage for her son. As long as she was in Russia while he was a prisoner in Mexico he would not talk – and perhaps vice versa. She had come to believe that the assurances she had been given about attempts to rescue Ramon were a bluff: she explained to her friend – "they are people without souls – they kill you slowly as they are doing to me now!" It was true that in Moscow refugees from Spain were being treated with contempt once they were no longer useful: also Stalin would not want to upset America by sending agents to Mexico to rescue Mercader. Caridad found herself shouting as Sylvia Agelof had once done – "It's all lies!"

Some amateur efforts at rescue did seem to have been made: there were some letters in invisible ink discovered by the U.S. censorship; instructions in code discovered at the Mexican border in the luggage of a schoolteacher from New York. Nothing came of these. Caridad Mercader turned up in Mexico City again after the war: it was said that she had managed to charm the new head of the secret police, Beria. Her old friend Leonid Eitigon had by now been purged. Caridad was travelling with a companion who was described to Mercader as a "mannish sportswoman" called Carmen Brufrau: the two set up house together near Ramon's jail. They were said to have worked on a plan to have Ramon injected with bacteria and then abducted from the hospital of Contagious Diseases; but with his horror of disease Mercader doubtless found it difficult to co-operate. Perhaps he also remembered the ways in which the G.P.U. might give overdoses of bacteria: his usefulness to them had ended and at least he was safe in jail. He got on with his television repair work.

There is in fact no record of Caridad's visiting him in jail. She returned after a time to her native country, Cuba. Then she moved to Paris where she was said to have had a job for a time as concierge at the Cuban Embassy. Her friend Carmen Brufrau disappeared – she had turned out, inevitably, to be an agent of the G.P.U.

Towards the end of his time in jail Mercader was transferred to the new Reformatory on the outskirts of the city – a modern establishment with good workshops and a restaurant and a theatre. There he carried on his teaching of electrical engineering. He had a new girl-friend who drove to and from the jail in a large American car he had given her. Mexican prisoners are allowed to make money by their work and Mercader did carry on some trade with his repair business; but the bulk of his money came from his "family" outside – the G.P.U. or his fictitious father in Belgium.

He was visited by journalists from time to time. He would shout at them – "You are all scandalmongers!" One writer saw him in 1947 when he was thin and well-dressed and easily recognisable from photographs of the time of the assassination: then by 1959, when the same writer saw him again, he was heavy and middle-aged – a typical bourgeois. However he still closely resembled photographs of his mother.

In 1953 the question of parole came up – he had served two-thirds of his sentence and, under Mexican law, parole after such a time is a right rather than a privilege. But evidence had just been produced that he was not Jacques Mornard but Ramon Mercader – though he continued to deny this. Interest in his case revived: he showed signs of panic. If he were let out, it might be dangerous for him if it were established that he was Mercader. The official psychiatrist, Dr Quiroz, recommended that he should not be paroled for the reasons – "He believes that he achieved a high moral purpose by murdering; he believes that he remained a moral man after having assassinated; he does not feel any repentance for the crime; he believes that the death of Trotsky was of benefit to the working-class; he does not consider himself an assassin, or a magnicide, or as morally insane, or abnormal . . ."

Against this there was the advice of another psychiatrist, Dr Casao, who thought that the prisoner was socially dangerous only to the extent that all Communist were socially dangerous, and that to deny him parole would be to imply that a lot of dedicated politicians should permanently be locked up.

The court denied Mercader parole on the grounds that he had "not expressed any moral regrets for having committed the crime" and that he was "proud of his status as an enigmatic man". On appeal, a higher court agreed with the decision and added that it was difficult for a man to be granted parole if no one knew officially who he was.

The identification of Jacson/Mornard as Ramon Mercader was made by Dr Quiroz, one of the psychiatrists who had spent 900 hours with him. It had from the beginning been established that he was not Mornard the Belgian as he had said; that he was most likely a Spaniard; he had been heard to speak Spanish fluently, which originally he had said he could not do, and a letter from him had been intercepted which contained idiomatic phrases in the Catalan dialect. In 1950 Dr Quiroz went to Barcelona taking with him Jacson/Mornard's fingerprints; but the police told him that the records of political prisoners had been destroyed in the civil war. He went on to Madrid where an official of the Police Headquarters took the fingerprints and returned "exactly one minute and forty seconds later" with a set of Ramon Mercader's fingerprints which had been taken when he had been arrested in Barcelona in June 1935. These matched Jacson/Mornard's. How this set had been found so quickly was not investigated. Dr Quiroz assumed that either the Spaniards had known of the identity of the assassin all the time but for their own reasons had not wanted to divulge it until the time came when it no longer mattered and Dr Quiroz turned up of whose approach they had been warned; or possibly the finding of the fingerprints said to be Mercader's was a further arrangement made by whatever secret agency at the time it suited.

But Dr Quiroz also dug out photographs of the Mercader family which showed striking resemblances not only between Caridad Mercader and Jacson/Mornard but between him and

Mercader's brother and sister. Finally a man claiming to be Ramon's long-lost father even turned up in Barcelona – he was thin and distinguished and not sluggish as in Mornard's description – but then Mornard had been talking to psychiatrists. And when the old man was shown photographs of Jacson/ Mornard he claimed that that was his son. There were also the innumerable stories from the underworlds of Moscow, New York and Paris, of Mercader himself and of Caridad Mercader's boasting of her son's great deed, or lamenting his imprisonment.

There were many Spaniards, however, who must have known Ramon Mercader at the time of the Spanish Civil War and who would have known Jacson/Mornard in Mexico. None of these came forward to identify him. But this could be explained by the fear that such people would probably have that they would end up in quick-lime like Sheldon Harte or with their skulls bashed in by a pick-axe. The deciding evidence that Jacson/Mornard is almost certainly Ramon Mercader is that no one had troubled to deny it. This might still mean that it has just not suited anyone to deny it – but of such a kind is the evidence of all history.

A late story that has emerged from the shadows is that although it is undoubted that the assassin is the son of Caridad Mercader, she, before the First World War, did in fact have amongst her lovers a rich Belgian called Mornard. This story is either too good, or good enough, to be true.

Mornard/Mercader came out of jail in 1960. He went first to Moscow where, it is said, he received some recognition in person for his services to the U.S.S.R.: then to Prague, where he settled down again to his work as a radio and television mechanic. He had with him the girl-friend who had visited him in the Mexican jail; also, supposedly, one or two children. He – or someone like him – granted an interview to a journalist at the end of the 1960's in Prague; he was living in an apartment with his family. He said that he would talk about anything after the time of the assassination but about nothing before it. He stuck to this resolution in spite of large offers of money. When the journalist pleaded that he should at least say who he was, he said – "I killed Trotsky!"

He is said still to be alive in Prague or Moscow. He has contacts with the denizens of his demi-world who perhaps sometimes, like Shakespearian murderers, see people where they are not. He has never admitted who he is. For twenty years he was exposed to almost limitless official investigation and at the end it was established that he was a Communist with a complex about his mother and his father – not much else: except that, without a doubt, he killed Trotsky. This was his mark in history. For the rest – the person – he seems just, as he himself would claim, an archetypal unidentifiable man who might or might not be a Belgian from Teheran, might or might not be a Spaniard with a Cuban mother, might or might not be the same man even now as the man who went into prison. If you are an agent of the G.P.U., or a modern political unit of population, or even an object in a criminologist's case-book, it doesn't matter – it's all the same – what matters is what you've done; and anyone can make what they like of you. And if you're someone who spent two years making love to a girl who didn't attract you for the purpose of at the end of it killing someone who probably did then you yourself might not even mind – might be glad to be put away for twenty years even – and when you came out just to have a job like mending television. Perhaps every now and then, when asked, you would look back through the mists of history and try to remember who you are – imagine your mother on the barricades or your wicked father in Belgium – you wouldn't be able to go back far because you would have become so accustomed to delusion – but you might sometimes remember the Old Man who, although you disagreed with him, at least knew who he was – always above everything he knew who he was – and by this he degraded you – and so you could smile and look up and could say – "I killed Trotsky!"

175

Chapter 21

Trotsky has been dead for thirty years but his name is still conjured with – almost literally, because although his story is lavishly documented (in Russia almost obliterated) and there are active political groups all over the world calling themselves Trotskyite and appealing to his authority as if he were still alive, there are still contradictions in his story that demand a leap of the mind. He is the other side of the coin from the blank tail of the assassin – the ineradicably recognisable lion's head with his pince-nez on his nose like balls. But he seems to contain these opposites within himself: he was the great revolutionary who spent his last years fighting the results of his revolution; the believer in history as a god who refused to accept his god's effects; the prophet of life and freedom who himself had had to dole out death; a thinker who saw the point and tragedy of these paradoxes and who went on honouring them till they killed him. He was a man of action and a man of reflection and he found it impossible to reconcile these two rôles: so he carried them both with him and in this sense did reconcile them: he went into exile, and poured out words. When he was young he created a victorious army and a Communist empire; when he was old he was closely protected in a bourgeois suburb. He seems not only to demonstrate but to be a model for the paradoxes of man – the hero who sees his hopes and achievements turn to dust but who does not give up and in the end even triumphs – not because he ever sees his expected results but because he has become a legendary and lasting protagonist in his own extraordinary story.

There is a part of Trotsky like Macbeth or Hamlet – he

started with some idea of what the world ought to be like and insisted that this was what it was like and then when it wasn't he was still committed. He lived at a time when old structures of mind were breaking up and old gods were dying and it was hoped that man himself might be some sort of god – but this man would still depend on a world outside him. Trotsky took Marx as his religion. Marx had said that history was going in a certain way and men had to go with it; a new type of man would then emerge that would be freed from any class that would oppress it. This would be a new type because without oppression it would not suffer from the sins of the old. Trotsky, like Marx, believed in the Working Class almost as other people believe in the Immaculate Conception – believed that after the Revolution there would in time be a classless society that would not be tainted with the greed, the idleness or the predatoriness that had for so long bedevilled classes; men would be able to get on rationally with building a just society. Why Trotsky believed this was a matter of faith; there was no evidence for it in history.

But part of Trotsky was always concerned with materialistic observation of life – with dialectics. At first he had combined this with his Marxist faith in history; it was then that he wrote of history itself living and moving by contradictions, of its deep-laid irony which it was "the duty of the historian or the artist to bring to the surface", of "the laws of revolution" which were "not accidental, but are subject to an objective necessity which is capable of theoretical explanation, and thus makes both prophesy and leadership possible". There was a rôle for the prophet and leader – but this was to explain and to minister to the necessities of history. "To understand the casual sequence of events and to find somewhere in the sequence one's own place – that is the first duty of a revolutionary." But what happened when the sequence of events in history did not seem to be going in the way that, in theory, the leader had explained it had to be going? The leader, as an expression of history, could not just say that he had been wrong. After a time, this was the dilemma of all Marxists.

In 1930 Trotsky had written – "A failure of correspondence between subjective and objective is, generally speaking, the fountain-source of the comic as also the tragic in both life and art. The sphere of politics less than any other is exempted from the action of this law. People or parties are heroic or comic not in themselves but in their relation to circumstances."

Circumstances were still the final arbiter. But what then, if leadership and prophesy failed, was the rôle of man?

"Events can neither be regarded as a series of adventures nor strung on the thread of some pre-conceived moral. They must obey their own laws. The discovery of these laws is the author's task."

There began to creep into Trotsky's remarks on these subjects more and more mentions of the rôle of writer or artist or discoverer – the man who might respect the laws of nature by trying to disclose them: not trying to impose on them, which was futile, but not being helpless in the face of them either, for by their disclosure circumstances and the laws themselves would be affected.

In his letter to the Founding Conference of the Fourth International in 1938 – even on such an important occasion – Trotsky had said:

"To prevent the shipwreck and rotting-away of humanity the proletariat needs a perspicacious, honest and fearless revolutionary leadership. No one can give this leadership except the Fourth International basing itself on the entire experience of past defeats and victories.

"Permit me, nevertheless, to cast a glance at the historic mission of the Fourth International not only with the eyes of a proletarian revolutionist but with the eyes of the artist which I am by profession. I have never separated these two spheres of my activity. My pen has never served me as a toy for my personal diversion or for that of the ruling classes. I have always forced myself to depict the sufferings, the hope and the struggles of the working classes because that is how I approach life, and therefore art, which is an inseparable part of it."

Trotsky was a great writer and a great orator; in these senses he was an artist but it did not seem to be just of this that he was speaking. The problem was – if Marxism as a faith in history failed, in what sense would the faith which he still had in his hard experience of Marxism be true? Trotsky had glimpsed the historical failure – the possibility that "the world proletariat should actually prove incapable of accomplishing its mission"; but in this case it would still be a Marxist's duty to "defend the interests of the slaves of the totalitarian bureaucratic system". But by what means and with what hope was this to be done? These should be continued political and polemical activity, certainly – none of Trotsky's reflections at this time interrupted the huge flow of his polemics – this was the constant exercise without which the body politic rotted. But whenever he stood back and considered the question of leadership, about which also the whole problem rotated, there seemed to be required some further understanding.

If the contradictions deep within history could not be reconciled within the structures of society they could still perhaps be reconciled in the activity of a person or persons who were the expressions of history. This was leadership. It was also a process usually thought to be aesthetic. But in practice, observing the material world and how it worked, what else was there to hope for? The rôle of a leader was to have the right vision.

When writing about Lenin in the 1917 revolution – although Trotsky had been at pains to insist that Lenin was in no way the creator of the revolution but just its most complete expression – Trotsky had said: "Besides other qualities, a great creative imagination was necessary to guide this work. One of the most valuable powers of imagination is the ability to visualise people, objects and events as they really are, even if one has never seen them. To combine separate little strokes caught on the wing, to supplement them by means of unformulated laws of correspondence and likelihood, and in this way to recreate a certain sphere of human life in all its concrete reality, basing everything on experience in life and upon theory – that is the imagination that a legislator, an administrator, a leader must have, especially in a period of revolution. Lenin's strength was chiefly this power of realistic imagination."

Towards the end of his life – as more and more the bureaucrats became the new ruling class and it became the duty of a true Marxist to defend the interest of their "slaves" – Trotsky tried to define what should be the characteristics of this revolutionary who would still be fighting for the workers. Here once more he turned for example and analogy to art. What was required, he said, if history would not be forced, was a struggle for truth – this was a man's effective contact with history.

In 1938 Trotsky had written of the "protest" necessarily inherent in any artistic creation: also of the necessity for art "to remain true to itself". Also:

"Not a single progressive idea has begun with a 'mass base', otherwise it would not have been a progressive idea. It is only in the last stage that the idea finds its masses – if, of course, it answers the needs of progress. The more daring the pioneers show in their ideas and actions – the more bitterly they oppose themselves to established authority which rests on a conservative 'mass base' – the more conventional souls, sceptics and snobs are inclined to see in the pioneers impotent eccentrics of 'anemic splinters'. But in the last analysis it is the conventional souls, sceptics and snobs who are wrong – and life passes them by."

Trotsky was all his life too much of a politician ever to say more than that politics and art could learn from each other – and that especially now, when it seems that political truth would have to be guarded by minority splinter-groups, politicians would have to learn from the nature of artistic activity. He never in any way, that is, advocated the renunciation of politics

180

for art – this would have been anathema to him. But he did seem to say that in the years when the blank-faced bureaucrats would be running the earth then the life of the true politician should have something of the solitariness and austerity and discipline of mind of the true artist – as well as the commitment. Without this, a politician would not be effective in history because he would not be true.

At the end of 1938 Trotsky wrote to André Breton – "The struggle for revolutionary ideas in art must begin once again with the struggle for artistic *truth*, not in terms of any single school, but in terms of *the immutable faith of the artist in his own inner self*. Without this there is no art. 'You shall not lie!' – that is the formula of salvation."

Since Trotsky's death there have been innumerable political splinter-movements of Trotskyites forming and breaking off from the Fourth International and re-grafting themselves until the parent stem is sometimes hardly recognisable. Trotsky had become accustomed to this sort of thing in his lifetime; he used to say, with irony, "Myself, I am not a Trotskyite!" To some of the actions of later groups he would have given his deep approval – there have been Trotskyite organisers behind demonstrations against the war in Vietnam; passionate protesters against other brutalities of Russian and American imperialism. About other sorts of activity he might have remarked, as he did about American splinter groups in the old days – "Their attitude to life is composed of shreds and fragments of the wisdom they absorbed in their student days; since they all have automobiles they are invariably elected to the important committees of the party." Much revolutionary activity is still carried on in the slanging-match style that occasionally bedevilled Trotsky himself.

The Fourth International has made little headway among the world's workers: perhaps Trotsky would have grown not to be surprised. He had begun to see that masses as masses did not change much; but the battle for change continues. The hopes of his "permanent revolution" seemed at one time to be being made flesh in China; where Mao, as soon as he saw a Stalinist-type bureaucracy rearing its ugly head, chopped it off by means of his own puritan Red Guards. But the heads of hydras grow again.

There are Trotskyite influences all over the world. The idea of permanent revolution – of a fight that has always to be carried on against the tendency for societies to divide between privileged and underprivileged – has taken root and has often taken the place of an older and more optimistic Marxism. But splinter groups continue to squabble and disintegrate amongst themselves.

Trotsky himself had turned his back on power almost somnambulistically in 1925. The question is sometimes asked – If Trotsky instead of Stalin had taken over power then in Russia would he have been forced to be as ruthless as Stalin was? But the question is no real question; Trotsky was not a man who in 1925 would have got power; he was too mercurial, too talented; he could not have settled to the rhythms of everyday politics that history seems to require – in terms of either cocktail parties or gratuitous killings. He had been a leader of exploits like Achilles: he retired to his tent. The man who took over, Stalin, was successful and rude on committees.

Stalin did his job – according to the particular rhythm of history. The workers' state was saved: the war was won. The cost was millions of men dying like mayflies.

Trotsky, from his exile, began to see that the way to influence the world if you choose to give up killing was perhaps just to become the exemplary character in your own lasting story. If you could not make the world do what you want it to do by telling it, you could go on telling it and at least make what you wanted of yourself. This was in your power; and might even influence the world because the world would recognise it.

Trotsky became the person with whose name for years people could magically conjure. By chipping away at the world he, like they, created an effect which was the living expression of his belief in permanent revolution. If the revolution did not occur as was required in the world it could exist in the pattern he made for himself and which others would follow. Trotsky knew about power: he knew also about the impossibility except at moments of combining power with dignity and freedom. Everything of importance had to grow; dialectics was a process both of man's evolution and that of history. The roots of dialectics were in nature; man was what they flowered into.

At Coyoacan Trotsky looked after his rabbits and tended his cacti and poured out his instructions for the salvation of the world. But it was not by forcing them that his rabbits or his Fourth International grew. A man worked hard according to the best scientific methods but in the end life had its own inner workings. A man's faith should be that there was some relation between his efforts and the outside world; but this was also his experience. The rhythms were similar; he could observe this, if not wholly explain it. But by this he could make, as Trotsky did, his passionate affirmations.

So when Trotsky sat at his desk on an August day in 1940 and the faceless silhouette followed him in with its black-and-grey trilby and its raincoat with the dagger sewn inside and the pistol and the ice-pick like a sickle he did not have to ask – who are you? or what do you want? – there were grey faceless men everywhere now, and if they wanted to they would get him. They were faceless and he was not – it was by this they would recognise him and want to kill him. But people had to die; he himself had been responsible for killing. The point was, whatever happened, that there should be some understanding and purpose. Trotsky perhaps admitted the faceless silhouette into his study just for this – to demonstrate that a person should behave with courage and with dignity, and by this to show some faith in the dignity of mankind. For the rest, it did not much matter. So Trotsky read the silhouette's article with politeness and disdain; did not worry too much perhaps when it rudely sat down or laid its mackintosh on the table: Trotsky had had to put up with a lot in his life, after all, in the way of insults and contradictions. And even when the faceless man took the ice-pick out of his pocket – the pick that might be useful for climbing mountains or smashing skulls or even breaking ice for cocktails – Trotsky still might not too much have worried; his brain was much bigger than most which was why the faceless man had to kill him; but with what he had made of it it would go on, and have its effect in the world outside him. This would be a permanency; and some sort of revolution. So even when the faceless man brought the pick down on Trotsky's skull Trotsky could still jump up and go after him roaring and bite him on the finger and say – "I prevented him!"

A NOTE ON SOURCES

For details of Trotsky's life and politics there is Isaac Deutcher's biography in three volumes – *The Prophet Armed*, *The Prophet Unarmed* and *The Prophet Outcast*.

For the two assassination attempts there are Colonel Salazar's book *Murder in Mexico* (written in collaboration with Julian Gorkin) and Isaac Don Levine's *The Mind of an Assassin*. The latter also gives stories of spies and saboteurs.

Trotskyite publishers continue to produce his books, pamphlets, articles and letters. In particular there are two collections of the *Writings of Leon Trotsky 1939–1940* and *1938–1939*: also a collection of "reminiscences and appraisals" called *Leon Trotsky The Man and his Work* which contains accounts by Natalya Sedova and two of Trotsky's secretaries of the assassination attempts. These collections are published by Merit Publishers of New York.

His *Autobiography* gives the best insight into Trotsky.

THE CONQUEST OF THE INCAS
by John Hemming

'Much the best book on the Incas since Prescott's, which it is entitled to supersede . . .'

£1.25 *Illustrated*   Philip Magnus, *The Sunday Times*

AKHENATEN: PHARAOH OF EGYPT
by Cyril Aldred

'Enthralling . . . Akhenaten, husband of Nefertiti and predecessor of Tutankhamen, remains one of the most fascinating figures in world history.'

75p *Illustrated*   *Daily Telegraph*

SEXUAL POLITICS
by Kate Millett

The seminal book in the struggle for women's rights. 'Supremely interesting . . . brilliantly conceived.'

60p   *New York Times*

WORLDS IN COLLISION
by Immanuel Velikovsky

A startling re-interpretation of the historical past based on the comparative study of ancient civilizations and literary traditions.
'A literary earthquake.'

60p   *New York Times*

ONE DIMENSIONAL MAN
by Herbert Marcuse

'The most subversive book published in the United States this century.'

45P   *Le Nouvel Observateur*

EROS AND CIVILIZATION
by Herbert Marcuse

Poses fundamental new questions about Freud's views on sexuality and their relevance to political behaviour in modern society.

45P

THE SECRET LORE OF MAGIC
by Idries Shah

'The author of this fascinating guide book to the occult has included the texts of all the major spell books and Grimoires in one volume for the first time.'

60p *Illustrated*   *Oxford Mail*

THE DEVIL'S PICTUREBOOK
by Paul Huson

A complete guide to the history and meaning of the 78 cards in the Tarot pack.

50p *Illustrated*

BOB DYLAN
by Anthony Scaduto

Unflinchingly honest biography of one of the great myth-makers of the Sixties.

60p *Illustrated*

Akhenaten: Pharaoh of Egypt

Cyril Aldred

The Pharaoh Akhenaten, who ascended the throne of
Egypt c. 1377 B.C. has inspired more theories than
almost any other figure of ancient times: he was "the
first individual in history"; his reign was one of the most
crucial in the history of ancient Egypt; the monotheistic
cult of sun-worship which he imposed and the new
capital he dedicated to the Sun God at Amarna, caused
a convulsion in Egyptian society. Under his patronage
a new naturalistic style flourished in the arts – a style
with no precedents and no successors.

Akhenaten has been widely regarded as a modern figure,
born long before his time. Now, after 17 years' research,
Cyril Aldred has provided a brilliant reappraisal of the
Pharaoh and his times.

ABACUS   75p

The Secret Lore of Magic

Idries Shah

Subtitled "Books of the Sorcerers", THE SECRET
LORE OF MAGIC is a unique compendium of the
sources of Western occultism. These 'grimoires' or
grammars of Black and White Magic range from the
key of Solomon to the Grimoire of Honorius the Great,
from simple spells to complex ceremonial magic, from the
creation of talismans to the invocation of spirits.
Translated from medieval French, Latin, Hebrew and
other languages, the books of the magicians are fully
explained in the author's comments, and profusely
illustrated with figures, charts and diagrams.

ABACUS   6op

Sexual Politics

Kate Millett

With the publication of SEXUAL POLITICS Kate
Millett was recognised as a founder member of the
struggle for women's rights. Her book stands beside
Germaine Greer's "The Female Eunuch" as a razor-
edged exposé of male domination and patriarchal bias in
every sphere of life: education, employment, family life,
religion and sex. Especially effective is her exposé of
sexism in literature, from D. H. Lawrence to Norman
Mailer, which will elicit a shock of recognition from
women everywhere.

ABACUS 6op

Bob Dylan

Anthony Scaduto

This is a big, superbly detailed and important biography
of the man who was one of the most powerful seminal
influences on the turbulent 1960's – a brilliantly gifted
Minnesota kid who came forth with a secret bag of
torments to write and sing those songs whose sounds and
ideas are today's household worlds.

ABACUS 60p

Worlds In Collision

Immanuel Velikovsky

WORLDS IN COLLISION is no less than a reconstruction of Earth's past, based on the theory that cosmic disturbances involving our planet have more than once profoundly influenced the course of civilisation in historical times.

Drawing on a rich profusion of sources, from the Book of Exodus to the astronomical charts of the Babylonians, from the texts of Taoism to the records of the Maya, from Nordic epics to Polynesian folklore, Dr Velikovsky concludes that a major series of catastrophes took place in the second millenium B.C., followed by another in the 8th century B.C.

ABACUS   6op